THE
VEGETARIAN
JAPAN
TABLE

THE VEGETARIAN TABLE

JAPAN

VICTORIA WISE

PHOTOGRAPHY BY DEBORAH JONES

CHRONICLE BOOKS ◆ SAN FRANCISCO

DEDICATION

For my parents, Hank and Ruth Jenanyan,
who always held me close with wide open arms
so that I might venture forth unafraid.

Library of Congress Cataloging-in-Publication Data:

Wise, Victoria.
The vegetarian table: Japan/by Victoria Wise;
photographs by Deborah Jones.
p. cm.
Includes index.
ISBN 0-8118-1565-X (hc)
1. Vegetarian cookery. 2. Cookery, Japanese. I. Title.
TX837.W55 1998
641.5'636'0952—dc21   97-34414
CIP

Book Design: Louise Fili Ltd.
Design Assistants:
Tonya Hudson and Lesley Hathaway
Food Styling: Sandra Cook
Food Styling Assistant: Allyson Levy
Photography Styling: Sara Slavin
Photography Assistants: Jeri Jones, Ondine Vierra

Props generously provided by
Fillamento and Genji Antiques, Inc.
(both in San Francisco)

Printed in Hong Kong.

Distributed in Canada by Raincoast Books

Chronicle Books
85 Second Street
San Francisco, CA 94105
Web Site: www.chronbooks.com

CONTENTS

INTRODUCTION

❖

IN THE WORLD OF COOKING, JAPANESE FOOD IS SPECIAL. The islands of its homeland, rising out of the Pacific Ocean, tucked off the east Asian mainland far across the Sea of Japan, remained sequestered for centuries. Then, as history would have it, in modern times Japan has become a crossroads for travel, transportation, economics, technology, and cultural exchange as those from the west leaned east and vice versa. In the process, Japanese cuisine also evolved into one that naturally straddles the globe between East and West.

I had the good fortune to reside in Japan for a while when I was a child. Though it was not a happy time for the adults, as a child, I carried forth no prejudice or preconception, only wonder and wide open eyes. The sights, smells, and sounds I encountered imprinted images in my sensory memory that continue to influence my work and life. To this day, the intricate pattern of a Japanese kimono, the makeup of a Noh actor, the calligraphy on a Japanese scroll, a Haiku poem, the presentation of a Japanese meal allow me pause and elicit a sigh of joy.

In particular, I have always loved the Japanese way with food. Quite the opposite of the American order-three-bags-full for $1.99, a Japanese meal satisfies in a different way. Whether it be for a child's lunch box, a family meal, or an elaborate tea ceremony, each bite is offered as a blessing to eating. And, with it so prettily arranged, who can resist taking leisure for a moment? Five bites and you're happy because your mind, eye, and soul are replete and your stomach is full enough but not too full.

It's true, times have changed since my childhood sojourn. In Japan, today, you can find fast food hamburgers at one stand and take-out espresso coffee a few steps away. Grocery shelves are stocked with quick fixes for favorite flavors and ingredients, just as are our Western markets. Home cooks use rice cookers so they may prepare the daily staple automatically.

Still, the Japanese aesthetic and manner of eating and dining abide, and vegetables and grains remain the outstanding ingredients of the cuisine. This proclivity for vegetables and grains is impelled not only by what's available but also by the historical tradition of strict vegetarian cooking, the Zen macrobiotic diet, which rigorously prohibits the use of any animal products, even eggs. Though by no means adhered to by the majority of the population, its health guidelines imbue the culinary consciousness of the cultures to the extent that a meal is not a meal without a bowl of rice or noodles surrounded or topped by several vegetable offerings.

The range of produce historically available for the Japanese table, while limited, has added immeasurably to our own modern cooking options. Bland but highly textured vegetables, like lotus root and okra; mildly bitter ones, like eggplant, fiddlehead ferns, and fava beans; a plenitude of earthy mushrooms; acerbic tastes from the mustard family; dried and fresh sea greens—these are no longer unheard of or regional specialty foods in America. Nor are noodles of buckwheat, yam, or bean, and rice that ranges from white to brown to old and new.

On their side of the world, Japanese cooks have done the same, incorporating European and New World foods, such as green beans, potatoes, capsicum peppers, squashes, to round out and fulfill the historical dishes based on soy products, rice, and offerings from the sea.

For this book, I have focused on tradition, but, in keeping with the spirit of Japanese adventuresomeness in all creative endeavors, I have included innovations in the vegetarian tradition. I hope the recipes and writing open a window onto a beautiful view and provide helpful instructions to make a delicious meal, in the Japanese style, of course.

VICTORIA WISE
OAKLAND, CALIFORNIA

BASIC INGREDIENTS AND SEASONINGS
FOR THE JAPANESE TABLE

TO THE WESTERN COOK, JAPANESE FOOD MAY SEEM MYSTERIOUS AND ODDLY COMPREHENSIBLE, ALL AT THE SAME TIME. That's because, though the compositions are not ordinary for Occidental cooking, Japanese dishes employ many ingredients familiar in North American kitchens today. The first approach to Japanese cooking is probably right through your pantry door! Perusing the larder, you may well find soy sauce, rice vinegar, sesame seeds, dried mushrooms, maybe nori seaweed or sake in the cupboard, perhaps miso paste and tofu in the refrigerator. If not, a quick trip to the supermarket will supply. Following is a list of the fundamentals to have on hand, along with descriptions of the herbs and spices particular to Japanese cuisine.

SOY-BASED INGREDIENTS

Soybean cultivation was brought to Japan from China at least four thousand years ago. The plant and its incredible potential for kitchen use were readily embraced by Japanese agriculturists and exploited by Japanese cooks. As human food, soy products must be lauded. Soybeans contain, along with calcium and essential vitamins, more protein, and protein of higher nutritional quality, than any other legume. Ironically, today by far the largest crop of soybeans, whether for human food, animal feed, or industrial use (soap, paint, plastics, ink), is grown in the United States even though Americans are only occasional users in the kitchen, except for soy-based margarines.

SOY SAUCE

Soy sauce is a fermented mixture of roasted soybeans, sea salt, wheat (usually), and water, along with fermentation aids (aspergillus mold first, then lactobacillus starter for the second stage of production). The resulting brew is one of the great table sauces of the world. In Asian cuisines, it's also a predominant seasoning for cooking.

Originally invented by the Chinese, soy sauce and the art of making it were brought to Japan by Buddhist monks during the time of their doctrinal migrations eastward about a thousand years ago. In Japan, soy sauce underwent modification to meet the needs and palates of Japanese cooks. Two basic kinds emerged, traditional *shoyu* and tamari. The basic difference between the two kinds is that tamari is wheatfree, using roasted barley as the grain element. This is a benefit for those who are wheat-intolerant. Otherwise, both kinds can be quite delicious. Soy sauces vary: some are thin, some thick, some lighter for cooking, others more refined and more complex tasting for saucing. Should you ever pay more? Most definitely. The pricier domestic and imported brands that claim to be "made with organic soybeans; spring water; pure, untreated sea salt; no additives; and aged at least one year" are, in fact, superior.

Tofu, or fresh soybean curd, is another soy product staple introduced to Japan from China. Japanese-style tofu comes in four types:

FRESH TOFU: Now common even in supermarkets, fresh tofu accounts for two of the types. One is the more pedestrian cotton or regular tofu. Cotton tofu is most like its ancestor (*dou-fu* or *teu-feu*, depending on the region of China and the transliteration in Cantonese, hence, *tofu* or *dofu* in Japanese), though not as firm and dry as its Chinese cousin. The second familiar type is silken tofu, and, as its name suggests, it is somewhat special. Smoother, lighter, and more delicate on the tongue than cotton tofu, silken tofu is particularly suitable for summer fare. Both kinds come in extra firm, firm, and soft textures, and both are usually packaged in water to keep the curd fresh and moist. As a fresh product, tofu is perishable. It should be stored in the refrigerator, submerged in water, and used within a few days for optimum flavor.

TOFU PUFFS (*ABURAGE OR USUAGE*): Thin cakes of deep-fried tofu that can be pried open and used as pouches for rice or vegetable fillings. The puffs can also be sliced or cubed and simmered in soups or stews. Tofu puffs are packaged dry, not in water. Sometimes you can find a bulk bin of them in Asian markets. They are, nonetheless, a fresh, not preserved product and should be stored in the refrigerator and used within a week.

GRILLED TOFU (*YAKIDOFU*): Cotton tofu that has been lightly pressed to release moisture, then grilled. The result is a tofu cake with a very firm texture and tan, spongy crust. Japanese cooks like to include yakidofu in soups and simmered dishes, but since it is not readily available, the recipes in this book don't call for it.

MISO

Miso (fermented soybean paste), though also originating from a Chinese concoction, has come to be essentially Japanese. It is one of the most ingenious kitchen derivations of the soybean. Miso combines all the health benefits of any soybean product in a savory, all-purpose paste for flavoring salad dressings, soup broths, and vegetable sauces. (Some even tout its prowess, like that of garlic and ginger, in preventing or obviating all kinds of ill health from stomach upsets to cancer.) Culinarily, miso can replace pesto, tapenade, even nut butters as a vegetarian dollop on crackers, potatoes, celery ribs, or serve as a satisfying lick off the spoon all on its own.

There's a befuddling array of brand names, colors, and Japanese and English names on the labels of containers of miso. It's all the more puzzling for the novice because, as with wines, types describe both varietals and blends. For the sake of coherence, misos can be categorized as three basic kinds, with lots of variations. Soybeans are the essential ingredient, except in the very specialized all-barley miso. A miso blend can include rice or barley or be pure soybean. The mixture, aging process, and quality of ingredients all determine the texture, taste, and color. The three most common misos, all including rice, are:

RED MISO (*AKA MISO*): Rural miso, salty, with a hearty, earthy flavor.

WHITE MISO (*SHIRO MISO*): So-called temple miso, sweeter than red miso because it includes proportionally more rice and less salt; it is less aged and more expensive than red miso.

YELLOW MISO (*SHINSU MISO*): Smooth and salty, aged quickly, the least expensive and the most readily available in U.S. supermarkets.

In addition, there are many specialized misos, rarely available in the United States. Two are:

BROWN MISO (*HATCHO MISO*): All soybeans, no grain, with a deep color, robust flavor, and dense texture; long aged, most expensive.

BARLEY MISO (*MUGI MISO*): All barley, no soybeans, long aged, chunky.

Since miso is a fermented product, it is not highly perishable so long as it's not subjected to intense heat and sunlight. Grocery stores usually stock miso on the shelf, not in the refrigerator section. At home, though, I store miso in the refrigerator to ensure long-term freshness.

FRESH SOYBEANS

Pervasive as processed soybean products are in Japanese cooking, it seems fresh soybeans are reserved for treat food. They are sometimes shelled and roasted for snacking, much like peanuts, or boiled whole in the pod for munching while awaiting dinner. Unfortunately, fresh soybeans still in the pod are rarely available unless you grow them or know someone who does, but sometimes you can find them in a specialty market, in the freezer section. See page 28 for how to prepare them.

DRIED SOYBEANS

Dried soybeans come in two colors, black and yellow. In Japan, neither is considered substance for full-meal fare. Rather, cooked dried black soybeans appear three or four at a time as an accent in a savory rice dish, or, more usually, they're turned into a sweetened dessert concoction, usually with chestnuts, to eat on their own like a sweet preserve or to top ice cream. Yellow soybeans are mostly employed for making secondary soybean products like soy milk, flour, or curd, presumably because their lighter color doesn't taint the finished product an unappealing gray. Though pretty as pearls, yellow soybeans are rarely available and are not normally used in the Japanese home kitchen, so the recipes in this book do not call for them. Black soybeans, on the other hand, can be treated similarly to more familiar Western dried beans and are called for.

To cook dried black soybeans, soak 1 cup dried beans in 4 cups water overnight. (The quick soak method doesn't work for these; they must be soaked overnight.) Place the beans and the soaking liquid in a pot, bring to a boil, and simmer briskly, partially covered, for 3 to 4 hours, or until the beans are tender. At the end of each hour, stir and add enough water to have the beans float again. When the beans are tender, stir in ½ teaspoon salt. Use right away or cool and refrigerate in the remaining liquid. (Cooked soybeans will keep in the refrigerator for up to 1 week.)

SOYBEAN SPROUTS

The sprouts of fresh soybeans, though popular in Chinese dishes, are seldom used in Japanese cooking. Japanese recipes tend to call for mung bean sprouts (plain old bean sprouts) for cooked dishes or daikon sprouts for uncooked garnishing.

OTHER SOYBEAN INGREDIENTS

There are numerous other soybean-based ingredients special to Japanese cooking, notably, freeze-dried tofu; soybean milk skin (*yuba*); and soybean curd pulp. Since I have endeavored in this volume to make the recipes accessible to beginners or those without a Japanese market, these ingredients are not called for.

OTHER OLD WORLD BEANS

It's true, the world had to wait for the age of exploration and the discovery of the New World to have lima and runner beans on the table. But long before, in addition to soybeans, mung, azuki, and fava beans were cultivated and eaten throughout Asia in savory and sweet preparations both. Like dried soybeans, mung, azuki, and fava beans are used in small amounts, even as individual beans, to add color and texture to composed dishes, or sweetened and pureed for the base of a dessert.

RICE

So eminent is rice at the Japanese table that its name in Japanese, *gohan*, is also the name for the meal. And so important is rice for nutrition and dining satisfaction both that no meal is complete without it. Rice provides the weft and warp around and through which all other elements of food and dining are interlaced. Much of the very limited agricultural space in Japan is given over to the cultivation of rice. Short-grain, or pearl rice, is the kind used, but the story doesn't stop there. There are crop differences you might not notice if you did not have the Japanese esteem for rice. Much as the first fruits of spring—cherries and apricots—are more loudly acclaimed than the same old banana or wintered-over apple, new rice is a prized product. It's moist, sweet, and fresh. Still, old rice never loses its status as a staple of the kitchen and of life year-round. Come winter, its glory as an ever-available element of nutrition and dining pleasure is once again praised. The recipes in this book call for short-grain white rice, the kind always found on grocery store shelves, and the kind Japanese cooks prefer. Cooking differences between new and old, white and brown, rice are given on pages 53-55.

RICE FLOUR

There are two kinds of rice flour: *shiratamako*, which is made of uncooked ground sweet rice and is the more refined, and *mochiko*, which is ground after the rice is cooked and dried. While the former is preferred for its fineness, the more available mochiko, which you can find boxed on most supermarket shelves, works just fine for the rice dumpling recipes in this book, sweet or savory (page 124).

SEA GREENS

The Japanese are masters at harvesting sea greens from the waters that surround their islands and turning them to culinary use. There is probably not a nation in the world that has so explored and refined the use of Neptune's vegetables. Descriptions and recipes for each could comprise an entire volume. For ease and accessibility, the recipes in this book call only for the most familiar sea greens that come dried and packaged: roasted nori seaweed, kombu kelp, and wakame seaweed. All are available in many supermarkets, with the occasional foray to a specialty store.

FIELD GREENS

Field greens in Japanese cooking take second place to sea greens. For the Japanese table, those employed include mainly spinach and some of the cabbage family (brassicas), such as head cabbage and celery cabbage (napa cabbage), and the leafier members of the cabbage family like mizuna and mustard greens. The heartier stem and flowering head cabbages such as all the choys and broccoli, are not used to the extent they are in Chinese cooking.

KAMPYO

Kampyo, the shaved and dried strands of a Japanese gourd, look like untied raffia. They serve a double purpose in Japanese cooking. Softened in water, they're used as decorative ties; further simmered in a seasoned liquid, they're included as an ingredient in soupy dishes or *maki-sushi* filling. You can find packages of dried kampyo in Asian markets.

To prepare kampyo, rinse the strands and place them in a bowl. Sprinkle with salt and knead gently to soften them. Cover with water and set aside to soak for 10 minutes. Rinse and drain.

For softened kampyo, place the strands in a medium pot, cover with fresh water, and bring to a boil. Simmer for 10 to 15 minutes, or until quite pliable but not easily broken. Drain and cool, then cut the strands in half for use as ties for vegetables or tofu-puff purses.

For simmered kampyo, place the softened strands in a mixture of 1 tablespoon soy sauce, 1 tablespoon sugar, and 1¾ cups dashi (see pages 37-38). Bring to a boil and simmer for 5 to 10 minutes, until the kampyo begins to turn translucent. Drain and cool or chill. Stir into simmered dishes or layer in maki-sushi rolls.

MUSHROOMS

Mushrooms, both fresh and dried, are major players in Japanese cooking. From the peppery and stalwart shiitakes to the delicate, threadlike enokis, they provide an earthy taste and aroma as vegetable element, seasoning, or garnish in many a dish. Shiitakes, the quintessential Japanese mushroom, are widely available, dried, if not fresh. Many modern supermarkets carry other Japanese varieties now being cultivated in the United States. I regularly find fresh oyster mushrooms (sometimes called tree oyster mushrooms), dried tree ears (a different kind, sometimes called cloud ears), and vacuum-wrapped packages of enokis. In addition, mushrooms have become so popular, there is often a selection of fresh chanterelles, portobellos, porcini, and more that the mushroom-loving cook can use as substitutions in the recipes in this book.

The array of tastes used to flavor and finish a dish—salt, pepper, herbs, spices, oil, a dash of lemon or vinegar, a pinch of sugar—is common around the world. But the ingredients that provide the seasonings are not always the same. In Japanese cooking, these fundamentals of taste and texture remain, but the bouquet is differently comprised and arranged. Following is a list of basic seasonings for Japanese cooking, in alphabetical order.

GINGER

Ginger is a primary element in Japanese cooking and serves both as vegetable and spice. It is used fresh—sliced, grated, or very finely julienned, or pickled—not dried and powdered.

HERBS

The herbs of Japanese cuisine are unusual and surprising to the Western palate. They are also highly appealing. Unfortunately, Japanese herbs are not widely available. You must have a garden or specialty market to harvest from, but substitutions are given in the recipes. The basics include:

SHISO, ALSO CALLED PERILLA: A member of the mint family. Two varietals are used in Japanese cooking, green and red, with different applications. Green shiso is used whole to under- or over-leaf a sushi ball or cut into chiffonade to sprinkle on a rice or fish dish; red shiso is a must for fragrance and color in the Japanese pickled plums condiment, umeboshi. Shiso, of either color, is sometimes available in specialty markets. It is also quite easy to cultivate in your garden. Ordinary garden mint, not peppermint or spearmint, makes a suitable substitute for garnishing.

KINOME: The early leaves of the prickly ash tree, which also provides the pods that are dried and ground for sansho, or Japanese pepper, is virtually not available fresh. It is worth a mention because it is so special and so prized in Japan for cooking in the spring, the only time it's available there!

MITSUBA (TREFOIL): A member of the large parsley family (*umbelliferae*). Like parsley, trefoil is used fresh. It is very difficult to find, but young carrot or celery leaves are suitable substitutes.

In addition, tender watercress leaves, daikon sprouts, and chives serve for herb embellishment in Japanese dishes and all are available here.

MIRIN

A sweet rice wine reserved for cooking. Since the alcohol content of mirin is low, you can often find it on grocery store shelves in the Asian ingredients section rather than in a liquor store. If you can't find it, sake sweetened with a pinch of sugar suffices, though it does not provide the same depth of flavor.

MUSTARD

Japanese mustard, *karashi*, is hot powdered mustard mixed to a stiff paste, like wasabi. It is used to season salad dressings, dipping sauces, and vegetable preparations and as a condiment for noodle or miso soups. Japanese powdered mustard is often laced with a small amount of ground turmeric to brighten the yellow color. Otherwise, there is not a distinctive taste difference between the Japanese product and the hot powdered mustards you find on the spice rack in supermarkets. Mustard paste is always used sparingly and always the same day because the punch, which is the point, dissipates over time.

OILS

Never as forceful as the taste-me olive oils of Mediterranean cooking, oils in Japanese cooking are background, reserved for deep-frying or a drop of flavoring. When oil is called for, soy, safflower, or canola are the choices. The more strongly flavored peanut or corn oils, excellent for other uses, are too overpowering for Japanese cooking, and olive oil is out of the question. When a definite oil flavor is required, sesame oil is the one of choice; it is added in drops to a larger portion of a more bland oil, never used as a cooking or dressing medium on its own.

PEPPER

Pepper appears in somewhat unusual forms in Japanese cooking. The European favorite black pepper, *piper nigrum*, is not used, even though it grows wild in much of Asia. The Japanese prefer their spice heat from sansho, wasabi, mustard, or chili peppers and almost always as a garnishing or condiment rather than as a cooking ingredient.

CHILI PEPPERS: Capsicum, the consummately New World spice that has been adopted around the globe, shows up in Japan as *tagarashi*, a small, intensely hot pod. It is sometimes used fresh but is usually dried, in the form of chili flakes. Any small chili, such as serrano, jalapeño, or Thai chili, will do as a substitute for the Japanese version. Red chili flakes are fine as a substitute for the dried ingredient.

SANSHO: The pod of the prickly ash tree, sansho, is particular to Japanese cooking. It is not at all the same as the Sichuan pepper, though both are varietals of the same plant and each packs a punch similar to freshly ground black pepper. Sansho is added at table, not during cooking. It is available in small, green-capped shake-top jars.

SALT

As finely powdered crystals from the sea or as soy sauce, salt seasons virtually every savory dish of Japanese cooking. Nonetheless, it is used judiciously, to highlight flavors, not overpower them.

SESAME SEEDS

Both white and black sesame seeds are used with abandon by Japanese cooks. Indeed, most households have a hand sesame seed grinder that is one of the most used kitchen gadgets, employed on a daily basis. Sesame seeds are normally toasted before using, to bring out the flavor. The taste difference between the two colors is not enormous, though the white seeds are oilier and somewhat sweeter, the black ones a bit denser and more bitter-earthy in taste. For Japanese cooks, one of the main considerations of choice is looks. On a white or light-colored background, black sesame seeds are preferred; on a dark-colored background, white sesame seeds. Even with the special grinder, toasting and grinding sesame seeds may seem like a bother, but don't be tempted to substitute the preground sesame paste, tahini. It lacks the proper texture and fresh-ground aroma necessary for an authentic Japanese dish.

SHICHIMI (SEVEN-SPICE POWDER)

Shichimi, which means seven spices, includes a combination of dried red chili, sansho, citrus peel, nori seaweed, sesame seeds, black poppy seeds, and either hemp seeds or white poppy seeds. As with other spice blends each cook's proportions are a closely kept secret. Hemp seed seems to be essential in old recipes, though it is not legally available today. White poppy seeds are equally obscure, even for the specialty shopper. Premixed shichimi is widely available in a shake-top jar or tin.

If you'd like to make your own, I've tried a combination of 1 teaspoon red chili flakes, ½ teaspoon coarsely ground white peppercorns (in place of the sansho), 1 teaspoon minced orange zest, ½ teaspoon sesame seeds, ¼ teaspoon poppy seeds, and 1 teaspoon minced nori. It is a good improvisation, but only six spices. A *rokochimi!*

SUGAR

While not normally listed as a spice, sugar is so loved by the Japanese that I include it here to note the fact. Western-style sweet desserts are by and large not part of Japanese cuisine, but sugar is commonly used as a backstage seasoning in savory dishes. It is sprinkled sparingly, a pinch here and there, to tame wild greens, soften the salt of the seas, sweeten the old rice.

UMEBOSHI (PICKLED PLUMS)

Though called pickled plums, umeboshi are actually a variety of apricot that doesn't ripen to sweetness. To make use of the fruit, too puckery to eat out of hand, Japanese cooks have devised a delightful sour-and-salty fruity pickle preserve colored with red shiso leaves. So successful was the innovation that pickled plums have become part of the cupboard stock in every Japanese kitchen and a jar of them rests ready to use in numerous ways, from tucking into the center of an otherwise plain patty of rice to adorning a specially elaborate sushi plate. Umeboshi are available in Japanese markets and, sometimes, health food stores because of their reputation as a digestive aid.

WASABI

Nicknamed Japanese horseradish, although it's not botanically related, the pungent, tear-producing condiment paste made from the dried and powdered wasabi root is by now renowned among sushi lovers worldwide. Powdered wasabi is available in small, brightly labeled tins in most large supermarkets. It is also available premixed in tubes that hold a quick fix for the harried cook, although the premixed lacks the earthy taste of what you mix yourself.

THE TART TASTE

In Japanese dishes, the tart, or sour, taste stands somewhat outside the realm of most-reached-for seasonings. It appears suggestively rather than aggressively; it never predominates. Even pickles, a necessary component of every Japanese meal, are characteristically not sour. When a touch of sour is desirable for a dish, it is provided by:

RICE VINEGAR

Soft and mild, with an acidity less than cider or distilled white vinegar, far less than aged or fresh wine vinegars. Excellent rice vinegars are available on most grocery store shelves; look for those that are labeled pure, not presweetened. The most precious, expensive, mellow version is brown rice vinegar, available in health food stores. (In Japan it is used as a tonic.)

CITRUS

In the form of yuzu citron, a remarkably fragrant cousin of lemon and lime, prized for its zest. Yuzu is rarely, if ever, available. If you can find Meyer lemon, it makes a good substitute for the perfume, though it lacks the thick, easily zested peel of yuzu. Ordinary lemon will also do.

Throughout Japan, sake, or rice wine, provides a salutation to the meal, perhaps the liquid refreshment throughout the meal, and a seasoning for many of the dishes offered. From Shinto shrines to Buddhist temples—even those that strictly obey the canons of nonindulgence—to the humblest home, sake plays a major role in the kitchen and on the table. Its quality and price depend, much as grape wine, on the growing region and care taken in processing. Unlike grape wine, however, sake is not expensive to produce. To make sake, rice mixed with aspergillus mold is allowed to ferment briefly, not more than sixty days. Although Japanese sakes are government graded into three divisions—special, first class, second class—since it is not a long-aged liquor, even the most refined sakes of rice from the finest paddies and water from the purest mountain streams are affordable. Also, a little goes a long way, both for cooking and imbibing. The alcohol content of sake is around sixteen percent, quite a bit higher than wine, and the custom of serving it warm to release the flavors also releases the vapors, which can go to your head rather rapidly. For those who mind, sake for cooking can be preheated to evaporate the alcohol.

CHAPTER ONE

APPETIZERS
AND
CONDIMENTS

TANTALIZING TIDBITS TO DRESS OR MAKE THE MEAL

SAVORY TIDBITS THAT NORMALLY SERVE AS APPETIZER OR HORS D'OEUVRES IN WESTERN DINING PLAY A DIFFERENT ROLE AT THE JAPANESE TABLE. Rather than meal starter, such delectables, along with a heaping bowl of rice, often constitute the meal. This chapter includes a selection of such tidbits to begin, garnish, or make a meal, Japanese or Western style. The dishes run the gamut from traditional to modern and include the customary pickles that are integral to almost every Japanese meal plus three modern salads.

PICKLED CUCUMBER

A SMALL SERVING OF CRUNCHY, MILDLY SALTY, PICKLED CUCUMBER APPEARS AT ALMOST EVERY JAPAN-ESE MAIN MEAL. STRAIGHTFORWARD AND UNADORNED, IT MANAGES STILL TO BE UNIVERSALLY APPEALING, THE FIRST DISH TO TASTE EVEN FOR ONE UNFAMILIAR WITH THE REST OF THE FARE. JAPANESE CUCUMBERS ARE THE FIRST CHOICE. THEY HAVE A MOST INTENSE CUCUMBER FLAVOR, REMINISCENT OF WATERMELON, A BOTANICAL COUSIN, PLUS THE ADDED ADVANTAGE OF BEING VERY TENDER AND SMALL-SEEDED SO YOU DON'T NEED TO PEEL OR SEED THEM. PICKLING OR REGULAR CUCUMBERS ARE ALSO FINE, BUT IF THEY ARE SEEDY, CUT THEM IN HALF LENGTHWISE AND SCOOP OUT THE SEEDS. ENGLISH, OR HOT-HOUSE, CUCUMBERS DO NOT DO WELL AS THEY LOSE TOO MUCH OF THEIR DELICATE FLAVOR IN THE PICKLING. THE OPTIONAL RED RADISH GARNISH, THOUGH NOT TRADITIONAL, PROVIDES COLOR AND EXTRA BITE.

Trim the ends off the cucumbers and slice them into very thin rounds. Place the slices in a bowl and sprinkle with the salt. Toss and knead the cucumbers until very juicy, about 1 minute. Cover with a plate that fits well inside the bowl so that it can sink as the cucumbers wilt. Place a weight, such as a heavy can, on top of the plate and set aside for 1 hour.

Drain the cucumbers, gently squeezing out the juice without wringing dry. Use right away or refrigerate for up to several hours. To serve, mound the cucumbers in a bowl and top with the radish, if using.

1 pound cucumbers, preferably Japanese or pickling cucumbers, scrubbed

2 teaspoons sea salt

2 tablespoons minced or coarsely grated red radish (optional)

PICKLED CABBAGE

WHEN IT COMES TO CABBAGE FOR JAPANESE COOKING, THE BEST CHOICES ARE NAPA CABBAGE, ALSO KNOWN AS CHINESE OR CELERY CABBAGE, AND REGULAR CABBAGE. NAPA CABBAGE IS MORE POROUS AND WATERY AND WILL PICKLE PROPERLY IN ABOUT ONE HOUR. REGULAR CABBAGE TAKES ABOUT TWO HOURS. THE RED CHILI PEPPER, A TYPICAL SEASONING OF KOREAN AND CHINESE PICKLED CABBAGES, IS ALSO MUCH USED IN NORTHERN REGIONS OF JAPAN, THOUGH NOT SO MUCH FROM TOKYO AND SOUTHWARD, WHERE THE CABBAGE PICKLE TENDS TO BE SIMPLY SALT-WILTED AND UNGARNISHED. IF YOU LIKE THE HEAT CHILI PROVIDES, YOU CAN TOSS IT IN WITH THE CABBAGE AND THE SALT IN THE FIRST STEP TO INFUSE THE MIXTURE AS IT PICKLES.

1 medium (1½ pounds) green or napa cabbage, quartered, cored, and finely shredded

1 tablespoon sea salt

½ teaspoon minced fresh red chili (optional)

Place the cabbage and salt in a large bowl. Toss together and knead the mixture with your hands until juices are released, about 1 minute. Scoop the cabbage into a mound and cover with a plate large enough to cover most of the surface but small enough to fit well inside the bowl. Top with a weight, such as a heavy can. Set aside until well wilted but still crunchy, 1 to 2 hours.

Drain the cabbage and squeeze out most of the liquid without wringing dry. Transfer to a serving dish or individual plates, sprinkle the red chili over the top, if using, and serve right away. (To store the cabbage pickle, drain it briefly and refrigerate for up to several days. Squeeze out the extra moisture when ready to serve.)

TURNIP PICKLE WITH TURNIP GREENS AND LEMON ZEST

❧

MAKES 3 CUPS

TURNIPS, LIKE BEETS AND CARROTS, USED TO COME WITH THEIR LEAFY GREEN TOPS INTACT. THESE DAYS, THE GREENS ARE ALL TOO OFTEN ALREADY TRIMMED OFF. WHILE THE TURNIP PICKLE CAN DO WITHOUT THEM, IT'S EVER SO MUCH BETTER WITH. FORTUNATELY, YOU CAN PURCHASE THE TOPS SEPARATELY, BUNCHED AS TURNIP GREENS.

Cut the tops off the turnips. Sort through the tops and discard any yellowed leaves and stems. Select the best-looking leaves and stems, rinse well, and cut into ½-inch-wide strips.

Bring a medium pot of salted water to a boil. Add the turnip tops and stems and, using a long-handled wooden spoon, push them into the water. Gently swish them about until wilted but still bright green, about 30 seconds. Drain in a colander, rinse under cold water, and set aside.

Peel the turnips. Cut the stem and bottom end off each turnip. Set each turnip, flat side down, on a cutting board and slice as fine as possible to make thin disks. Transfer the turnip slices to a large bowl.

Gently squeeze the turnip tops to rid them of extra moisture. Add them to the bowl with the turnip slices. Add the lemon zest, salt, and lemon juice. Toss and knead together until the mixture is very juicy, about 1 minute. Cover with a plate that fits well inside the bowl so that it can sink as the vegetables wilt. Place a weight, such as a heavy can, on top of the plate. Set aside for 2 hours, or until the turnips are thoroughly wilted but still crunchy. The pickle may be refrigerated, but no longer than 2 hours more.

Drain the turnips and greens and gently squeeze out some of the moisture without wringing dry. Mound in a bowl or on individual plates and serve right away.

1½ pounds turnips with tops or
*   1 pound topped turnips plus a small*
*   bunch of turnip greens*
1 tablespoon very finely shredded lemon zest
1 teaspoon sea salt
1 tablespoon fresh lemon juice

PICKLED GINGER

HOMEMADE PICKLED GINGER DIFFERS FROM THE STORE-BOUGHT OR STANDARD RESTAURANT VERSION MAINLY IN THAT IT TASTES EVER SO MUCH MORE OF GINGER. TRUE, IT'S A BIT OF A BOTHER TO PREPARE—YOU NEED A SHARP KNIFE AND STEADY HAND TO SLICE THE KNOBBY RHIZOME AS THIN AS POSSIBLE. BUT, EVEN WITH UNEVEN SLICES THE RESULT IS SO REMARKABLE YOU MAY WANT TO KEEP A SMALL JAR ON HAND FOR THAT SPECIAL BITE, WHENEVER. IF THE GINGER IS VERY YOUNG, THERE IS NO NEED TO PEEL IT, JUST SCRUB.

½ pound fresh ginger

1 teaspoon sea salt

1 cup rice wine vinegar

3 tablespoons sugar

If using older ginger, peel. If using young ginger, scrub. Slice the cleaned ginger as thinly as possible into rounds and transfer the rounds to a medium bowl.

Place three cups water and the salt in a small saucepan and bring to a boil. Stir and immediately pour over the ginger slices. Set aside until the ginger softens, about 2 minutes. Drain, reserving ½ cup of the liquid in a medium bowl.

Add the vinegar, sugar, and ginger to the reserved liquid. Swirl to mix and set aside in the refrigerator for at least 3 hours, or, preferably, overnight.

Serve as a garnish or on a small side plate to accompany almost any dish. (Pickled Ginger keeps in the refrigerator for several weeks.)

MUSTARD·PICKLED EGGPLANT

❀

MAKES 1 CUP

AS A MATTER OF COURSE, FASTIDIOUS COOKS WILT EGGPLANTS WITH SALT TO LEACH THE BITTERNESS AND SOFTEN THE PULP BEFORE SAUTÉING. THE JAPANESE TREATMENT OF SALT-WILTING BUT NOT COOKING THE EGGPLANT, JUST A BIT OF MUSTARD STIRRED IN AND AN HOUR OR SO STANDING TIME, IS A REVELATION—A TENDER, UNCTUOUS EGGPLANT CONDIMENT, WITH NO OIL AT ALL.

1 pound eggplants, any kind

1 teaspoon sea salt

1 teaspoon powdered mustard

To prepare the eggplants, rinse them and trim off the caps. Slice Japanese or other long eggplants crosswise into ¼-inch-thick rounds. Cut globe eggplants into ¼-inch dice.

Transfer the eggplant to a large bowl, add the salt, and knead until moisture is released, about 1 minute. Scoop the eggplant into a mound and cover with a plate small enough to fit well inside the bowl but large enough to cover most of the surface. Top with a weight, such as a heavy can, and set aside for 30 minutes.

Sprinkle the mustard powder over the eggplant and knead briefly again to mix well. Cover and weight again. Set aside for at least 30 minutes, or up to 2 hours, but not much longer. After that, the mustard loses its punch and the eggplant turns bitter.

Drain the eggplant and gently squeeze out some of the moisture without wringing it dry. Transfer to individual plates or mound on a platter and serve.

SAVORY SWEET WALNUTS

THE NUTMEAT OF THE WIDESPREAD WALNUT TREE, NATIVE TO BOTH EURASIA AND THE AMERICAS, HAS ESTABLISHED ITSELF AS AN INGREDIENT FOR MANY CUISINES. IN JAPANESE COOKING, THE OLD WORLD VARIETY, COMMONLY KNOWN AS ENGLISH WALNUT, APPEARS BRAISED OR FRIED, CHOPPED OR HALVED, AS A SAVORY APPETIZER AT FORMAL TEA CEREMONIES, DAILY TEMPLE MEALS, AND FAMILY TABLES. FOR THIS DISH, YOU CAN USE WALNUT PIECES INSTEAD OF HALVES, THOUGH THEY DON'T MAKE AS SPECTACULAR A PRESENTATION. BUT DO LOOK FOR NEW CROP WALNUTS, PREFERABLY ORGANIC, FOR THE FINEST RENDITION — OLD AND/OR STALE WALNUTS ARE TOO BITTER.

Combine the sake, sugar, and soy sauce in a medium nonreactive pan and bring to a boil. Add the walnuts and stir over medium-high heat until the walnuts are lightly browned and the liquid has evaporated, about 2 minutes. Transfer the walnuts to a plate and sprinkle the nori over the top. Serve right away. (The walnuts may be cooled, loosely covered with plastic wrap, and stored at room temperature for up to 3 days.)

3 tablespoons sake

2 teaspoons sugar

1 teaspoon soy sauce

1 cup (4 ounces) walnut halves

2 teaspoons finely shredded roasted nori seaweed

FRESH SOYBEANS BOILED IN THE POD

SERVES 4

FRESH SOYBEANS BOILED WHOLE IN THE POD MAKE A NIFTY SNACK OR APPETIZER. THE COOK DOESN'T EVEN HAVE TO SHELL THE BEANS. THE GUESTS DO THE WORK AS THEY MUNCH ALONG, USUALLY ALSO SIPPING SAKE.

8 ounces soybeans in the pod, fresh or
    frozen (see page 10)
2 teaspoons sea salt

Bring 2 quarts water to a rolling boil. Add the soybeans and salt, return to a boil, and cook for 6 minutes, or until the pods open easily and the beans are cooked but still al dente. Drain, rinse to cool, and serve.

MODERN SALAD OF ASIAN GREENS WITH RED MISO DRESSING

○

SERVES 6

PERHAPS CATERING TO WESTERN EXPECTATIONS, MANY MENUS IN AMERICAN JAPANESE RESTAURANTS NOW OFFER A SALAD OF FRESH GREENS, USUALLY HEAD LETTUCE, MIXED WITH OTHER FRESH VEGETABLES SUCH AS GRATED CARROT, AND DRESSED IN A JAPANESE WAY. THIS SALAD TAKES ITS CUE FROM SUCH PREPARATIONS, BUT WITH A SELECTION OF GREENS MORE IN THE JAPANESE TRADITION. YOU CAN CHOOSE FROM MIZUNA, TAT CHOI, WATERCRESS, BABY SPINACH, OR AN ALREADY MIXED VARIETY OF ASIAN GREENS WHICH YOU CAN SOMETIMES FIND IN GROCERY STORES. OR YOU CAN USE THE MORE READILY AVAILABLE NAPA CABBAGE EXCLUSIVELY. THE MISO DRESSING BRINGS THE SALAD INGREDIENTS TOGETHER IN A CUSTOMARY WAY.

Divide the greens and cabbage among 6 individual salad plates or bowls. Top with some of the carrots, apple, and scallions in separate piles on each plate or bowl. Drizzle the dressing over the top of each arrangement and serve right away. Or, place all the vegetables in a large salad bowl. Pour the dressing over the top, toss gently to mix, and serve.

4 cups (about 4 ounces) hearty Asian-style greens, washed and spun dry

½ medium head (about ¾ pound) napa cabbage, quartered lengthwise and coarsely chopped

2 medium carrots, scraped and coarsely grated

1 Fuji or Granny Smith apple, cut into eighths lengthwise, cored, and thinly sliced crosswise

4 scallions, trimmed and finely sliced lengthwise into 2-inch-long slivers

¾ cup Red Miso Dressing (recipe follows)

RED MISO DRESSING

○

MAKES ¾ CUP

Place all the ingredients in a small bowl and whisk until smooth. Use right away. (The dressing may be stored in the refrigerator for up to 1 week.)

½ cup red miso

½ cup water

2 tablespoons sake

1 tablespoon sugar

MELON, GREEN BEAN, AND DAIKON SALAD
WITH WASABI·LIME DRESSING

❂

SERVES 6

THOUGH BILLED AS TRADITION-BOUND IN MANY WAYS, THE JAPANESE ARE ALSO GREAT INNOVATORS. IN TECHNOLOGY, THE ARTS, AND THE KITCHEN, TOO, THE NEW IS EXPLORED, EXAMINED, AND INCORPORATED WHEN DESIRABLE. MELON, GREEN BEANS, AND DAIKON ARE USUAL IN JAPANESE COOKING. ASSEMBLING THEM AS IN THIS SALAD IS UNUSUAL, BUT IN KEEPING WITH THE JAPANESE SPIRIT OF MODERNITY.

6 ounces green beans, stem ends trimmed
   off, beans cut lengthwise in half
1 small (2 pounds) ripe but still firm
   honeydew melon, halved, seeded,
   peeled, and cut into ¼-inch dice
4 ounces daikon, peeled and coarsely
   grated or finely shredded
¼ cup Wasabi-Lime Dressing (recipe
   follows)

Bring a medium pot of water to a boil. Add the green beans, return to the boil, and cook until the beans are just tender but still bright green, 2 to 3 minutes. Drain, rinse with cool water, and shake dry.

Place all the ingredients in a bowl and toss gently. Serve right away, while the salad is fresh and crisp.

WASABI·LIME DRESSING

❂

MAKES ¼ CUP

2 teaspoons wasabi powder
2 tablespoons fresh lime juice
¼ teaspoon sea salt
¼ teaspoon sugar

Whisk together the wasabi powder and 2 teaspoons water in a small bowl. Set aside for 5 minutes.

Stir in the lime juice, salt, and sugar. Use right away or set aside for up to 30 minutes but no longer. After that the dressing loses its punch.

SALTED WINTER TOMATOES WITH MITSUBA BOWS

◆

SERVES 6

TOMATOES DO NOT APPEAR IN JAPANESE DISHES, EXCEPT, PERHAPS, OCCASIONALLY AS A WEDGE TO GARNISH A MODERN SALAD IN AMERICAN JAPANESE RESTAURANTS. COOKED TOMATOES ARE UNHEARD OF. STILL, FIRM PINK AND GREEN — NOT JUICY RED — TOMATOES COULD PLEASE A JAPANESE GUEST AND, SINCE I CAN'T LIVE WITHOUT TOMATOES, I DEVISED THIS WHIMSICAL, ULTRA-MODERN SALAD FOR THE JAPANESE TABLE.

2 medium, very firm, slightly green
tomatoes
¼ teaspoon sea salt
12 mitsuba (trefoil) stems, roots
pinched off

Cut each tomato into 6 rounds and arrange the slices on a plate. Sprinkle the salt over the tomatoes and set aside.

Bring a small pot of water to boil. Swirl in the trefoil stems, drain immediately, and rinse under cool water. Tie each stem into a bow and garnish each tomato slice with a bow. Serve right away.

CHAPTER TWO

SOUPS

KOMBU KELP DASHI

KELP DASHI IS USED MAINLY FOR CLEAR SOUPS. ITS TASTE, LIKE FRESH SEA WATER, IS QUITE PRONOUNCED TO PALATES UNUSED TO COOKING WITH SEA VEGETABLES. COOKS ARE DIVIDED BETWEEN TWO METHODS FOR MAKING KELP DASHI—LONG STEEPING OR QUICK COOKING? SOME CLAIM THAT COOKING PRODUCES A LESS FRESH FLAVOR, MORE ON THE BITTER SIDE, AND SO THE KELP SHOULD BE STEEPED WITHOUT BENEFIT OF HEAT. OTHERS AVOW THAT RAPID BOILING RESULTS IN A LESS GLUTINOUS, MORE DESIRABLE BROTH. BOTH CLAIMS ARE TRUE, AND YOU MAY SUIT YOURSELF. EITHER WAY, ALL AGREE: THE KELP, ALWAYS USED DRIED, SHOULD BE GENTLY WIPED TO RID IT OF DUST, NEVER THOROUGHLY RINSED. THE WHITE POWDER COATING IS PART OF ITS FLAVOR.

16 inch piece (2 ounces) dried kombu kelp (see page 11)

Wipe the kelp with a damp cloth or paper towel and break it into about 3-inch pieces.

TO COOK THE KELP: place the kelp pieces in a medium pot. Add 6 cups water and bring to a boil. Reduce the heat to a gentle simmer, partially cover the pot, and cook for 20 minutes, or until the kelp is soft and pliable and the liquid is reduced by a quarter.

TO STEEP THE KELP: place the kelp pieces in a large bowl. Add 6 cups water and set aside to steep for 4 hours.

Whichever method you have used, remove the kelp and reserve it for another dish. Use the dashi right away. (Dashi may be stored in the refrigerator for up to 3 days.)

NOTE: The kelp pieces from the first or "primary" dashi, meaning the first steeping, are customarily used again to make a "secondary" dashi. Vegetables and often bonito flakes enrich the second-round broth, which is used for miso soups, noodle dishes, and other seasoning needs.

MISO SOUP

❖

A BOWL OF MISO SOUP WARMS THE HANDS, WHETS THE APPETITE, BRACES THE DAY. It also calms the spirit and restores at any time. for all this, miso soup is the essence of simplicity: start with a good dashi, stir in miso paste, and float two or three vegetable bits for beauty and completeness. There, you have a healthful elixir of protein and comfort.

RED MISO SOUP

❖

SERVES 4

IN THE CLASSIC, AND MOST COMMON, VERSION OF MISO SOUP, SHIITAKE MUSHROOMS PROVIDE A TOUCH OF FANCY TO THE EVERYDAY RED MISO AND TOFU.

3½ cups Vegetable Dashi (page 37)

3 to 4 tablespoons red miso

½-inch-thick slice (about 4 ounces) soft
 tofu, cut into ½-inch cubes

4 stems mitsuba (trefoil), chopped, or 1
 scallion, trimmed and cut into
 2-inch-long slivers

2 fresh shiitake or equal amount other
 fresh mushrooms, rinsed, stemmed,
 and cut into ¼-inch slices

Put the dashi in a medium pot or microwave bowl and bring to a boil. Place the miso in a small bowl, add ½ cup of the warm dashi, and whisk to smooth. Set aside.

Divide the tofu and trefoil among 4 individual bowls and set aside.

Add the mushrooms to the dashi and simmer until soft and heated through, about 1 minute. Stir in the miso mixture, taking care not to let the liquid boil again. Ladle the broth and mushrooms into the bowls and serve right away.

WHITE MISO SOUP

✿

SERVES 4

WHITE MISO, SOMETIMES CALLED TEMPLE MISO, IS SWEETER THAN RED AND MORE EXPENSIVE. IT IS THE KIND PREFERRED IN BUDDHIST AND KAISEKI (ZEN BUDDHIST) COOKING, AND FOR COMPANY.

Place the tofu puffs slices in a colander and pour boiling water over them. Set aside.

Put the dashi in a medium pot or microwave bowl and bring to a boil.

Place the miso in a small bowl, add ½ cup of the warm dashi, and whisk to smooth. Set aside.

Add the tofu puff slices and leeks to the dashi and simmer very gently for 2 minutes, until wilted. Stir in the miso, taking care not to let the liquid boil again. Ladle into soup bowls, dividing the ingredients equally. Garnish with the lemon zest and serve right away.

8 thin slices tofu puffs (aburage), or 4 ounces soft tofu, cut into ½ inch cubes

3½ cups Vegetable Dashi (page 37)

1 small or ½ large leek, white part only, trimmed and sliced into very thin rounds, well rinsed

5 to 6 tablespoons white miso

12 strands (1½ inches long) of lemon zest

MISO SOUP VARIATIONS

✿

MISO SOUP NEED NEVER BE HUMDRUM. IN ADDITION TO THE CLASSIC ELEMENTS AND THOSE CALLED FOR IN THE PRECEDING RECIPES, MANY INGREDIENTS ARE USED TO VARY THE DAILY BOWL. WHEN MIXING AND MATCHING INGREDIENTS, CONSIDER VISUAL APPEAL. THE COOK WITH AN EYE TO BEAUTY WILL BALANCE A BEIGE OR BROWNISH ELEMENT WITH A MORE COLORFUL ONE IN THE ORANGE OR GREEN RANGE. THE FOLLOWING INGREDIENTS, INCLUDING SOME ESOTERIC ONES AVAILABLE ONLY IN JAPANESE MARKETS, SUIT MISO SOUP IN ANY SEASON:

AZUKI BEANS, cooked (see page 119)

CABBAGE, finely shredded

CARROT, thinly sliced into flowers or ovals and parboiled

DAIKON, cut into rounds, half moons, or julienne strips, and parboiled; this is a good use for the daikon pieces strained from making Vegetable Dashi (page 37)

KAMPYO, reconstituted in water and tied into bows or decorative knots

SWEET POTATO, peeled, thinly sliced, and parboiled

GRILLED TOFU, (yakidofu), reconstituted in water

RED AND WHITE MISO SOUP
FOR ALL SEASONS

❦

SERVES 4

RED AND WHITE MISO SOUP COMBINES THE COMMON WITH THE EXALTED IN A BOWL. BLACK BEANS, GREEN SPINACH, AND YELLOW MUSTARD, ALWAYS AVAILABLE, ENSURE AN ARTFUL JOINING FOR ALL SEASONS.

½ teaspoon mustard powder

12 cooked dried black soybeans (see page 10)

¼ cup shredded spinach leaves, blanched and drained

3½ cups Vegetable Dashi (page 37)

1 tablespoon red miso

2 tablespoons white miso

Whisk together the mustard powder and ½ teaspoon water in a small bowl. Set aside. Divide the beans and spinach among 4 serving bowls, keeping them in separate piles. Place a tiny dollop of mustard paste to the side of the vegetables in each bowl and set aside.

Heat the dashi in a medium pot or microwave bowl until boiling.

Place the red and white miso in a medium bowl, add ½ cup of the hot dashi, and whisk until smooth. Whisk the dissolved miso into the hot dashi, taking care not to let the liquid boil again. Ladle the mixture into the serving bowls and serve right away.

CLEAR SOUPS

❀

THE CLEAR SOUPS OF JAPANESE CUISINE ARE AKIN TO THE BOUILLONS AND CONSOMMÉS OF WESTERN FARE AND, LIKE THEM, OFFER A SOPHISTICATED TOUCH TO THE MEAL RATHER THAN PROVIDING A SUBSTANTIVE FORCE. In a clear soup, a bowl of dashi, lightly seasoned with soy sauce and sake, holds a mere two or three ingredients, just enough for eye appeal and toothsomeness without clouding the sublime clarity of the broth.

CLEAR SOUP WITH CABBAGE AND SWEET POTATO

❀

SERVES 4

A WARMING WINTER SOUP OF HEARTY INGREDIENTS, CABBAGE AND SWEET POTATO, IS DELICATELY AND DECORATIVELY RENDERED IN JAPANESE STYLE.

Bring a medium pot of water to a boil. Drop the watercress sprigs into the pot and remove immediately with a slotted spoon. Set aside.

Add the sweet potato slices to the boiling water and simmer briskly until cooked but still holding their shape, about 4 minutes. With a slotted spoon, transfer the slices to a colander and set aside.

Cut the cabbage lengthwise in half or quarters, depending on the size, to make about 2-inch-wide sections. Cut out the core from each section and slice the cabbage leaves crosswise into thin shreds. Parboil the cabbage in the boiling water until wilted but not cooked through, about 1 minute. Drain and set aside.

Combine the dashi, soy sauce, sake, and salt in a medium pot or microwave bowl and heat until almost boiling.

Arrange a mound of cabbage and 2 yam slices in each of 4 serving bowls. Ladle the broth into the bowls, set a watercress sprig in each, and serve right away.

4 large sprigs of watercress, thick stems removed

4 ounces sweet potato or yam, peeled and sliced into eight ⅛-inch-thick ovals

½ small or ¼ large head (8 ounces) napa cabbage

3½ cups Vegetable or Kombu Kelp Dashi (pages 37-38)

1 teaspoon soy sauce

2 teaspoons sake

1½ teaspoons sea salt

SHIITAKE AND ENOKI MUSHROOM CLEAR SOUP IN GINGER BROTH

SHIITAKE MUSHROOMS AND GINGER SIMMER INTO AN IRRESISTIBLE BROTH FOR A CLEAR SOUP. GARNISHED WITH SCALLION-WRAPPED BUNDLES OF ENOKI MUSHROOMS, A BOWL OF IT IS FIT TO SERVE THE MOST HONORED GUESTS, AND IT'S EASY ON THE COOK. THE BROTH ALONE, WITHOUT THE ELEGANT GARNISH, SERVES AS DASHI FOR OTHER CLEAR AND MISO SOUPS, HEALTHFUL IN EVERY WAY.

6 medium (3 to 4 ounces) fresh shiitake
    mushrooms (see Notes)
3 tablespoons coarsely chopped fresh
    ginger
½ teaspoon sea salt
4 scallion tops, at least 9 inches long
2 ounces enoki mushrooms
1 tablespoon sake
2 teaspoons soy sauce

Wipe or rinse the shiitake mushrooms and trim off the stems. Select four of the nicest looking caps and set them aside. Coarsely chop the stems and remaining caps.

Place the chopped shiitakes, ginger, salt, and 8 cups water in a medium pot. Bring to a boil and simmer, uncovered, for 15 minutes. Drain the liquid into a clean pot and bring back to a boil. Drop in the scallion tops and remove immediately with a slotted spoon. Set the scallions aside to cool and remove the pot from the heat.

Trim away the bottom ends of the enoki mushrooms and divide into 4 clumps. Tie each clump with a scallion to make 4 bundles and place 1 bundle in each of 4 individual bowls.

When ready to serve, add the sake and soy sauce to the shiitake-ginger broth and bring back to a boil. Add the reserved shiitake caps and simmer until soft, about 2 minutes. Lift out the caps with a slotted spoon and place one in each bowl alongside the enoki mushroom bundles. Ladle the broth into the bowls and serve right away.

NOTES: Six dried shiitakes may be substituted, but they must be soaked in 1 cup warm water for 20 minutes so that they are quite pliable before proceeding with the recipe. Use the soaking water in place of 1 cup of the plain water when making the broth.

Whole shiitake mushroom caps make a lovelier presentation, but for ease of eating, you may wish to cut the caps into halves or quarters.

WAKAME SEAWEED AND TOFU CLEAR SOUP

❀

SERVES 4

IN JAPAN, A CLEAR SOUP OF WAKAME SEAWEED AND TOFU NOURISHES THE WEARY WORKER AND THE HUNGRY CHILD ALIKE THROUGHOUT THE DAY. IT'S A CLASSIC, SO MUCH SO THAT ONE CAN FIND READY-TO-MIX PACKETS ON GROCERY STORE SHELVES. OF COURSE, HOMEMADE IS BETTER, AND IF THE DASHI IS READY TO HAND, THE SOUP IS A VERY QUICK MIX. YOU CAN SUBSTITUTE VEGETABLE DASHI FOR THE KOMBU KELP DASHI, THOUGH YOU DO SACRIFICE SOME OF THE AWAKENING FLAVOR AND FRAGRANCE OF THE CLEAR GREEN SEA.

¼ ounce (scant) dried wakame seaweed

4 ounces soft tofu, cut into 4 cubes

3½ cups Kombu Kelp Dashi (page 38)

1 teaspoon soy sauce

2 teaspoons sake

½ teaspoon sea salt

1 tablespoon finely shredded lemon zest

Cut the wakame into 1-inch lengths with a scissors. Place in a bowl with plenty of water to cover and set aside to soak until soft, about 10 minutes. Drain and set aside.

Place 1 tofu cube in each of 4 serving bowls and set aside.

Combine the dashi, soy sauce, sake, and salt in a medium pot or microwave bowl and heat until almost boiling. Stir in the wakame and ladle the soup into the bowls. Garnish with the lemon zest and serve right away.

SAVORY CUSTARD SOUP

⬥

THE SOFT AND SAVORY CUSTARD KNOWN AS *CHAWAN MUSHI* HOLDS A SPECIAL PLACE IN MY HEART. MY MOTHER, AN INTREPID WORLD TRAVELER AND ALWAYS THE EAGER COOK, LEARNED TO MAKE IT WHEN WE LIVED IN JAPAN. IN OUR FAMILY, ONE HAD THE LIBERTY, CONSIDERED A RIGHT, OF CHOOSING THE MENU FOR ONE'S BIRTHDAY. MY CHOICE WAS ALWAYS A JAPANESE MEAL, *CHAWAN MUSHI* TO START, PLEASE. A GREAT DEAL OF THE FUN WAS THE RITUAL PRESENTATION OF EACH DISH, ESPECIALLY THE *CHAWAN MUSHI*, SERVED, AS TRADITION DICTATED, IN LIDDED, DECORATED PORCELAIN BOWLS DESIGNED ESPECIALLY FOR STEAMING AND SERVING THE CUSTARD PIPING HOT. THE BOWLS, HAVING TRAVELED FAR AND WIDE, AS DID OUR FAMILY, ARE NOW SHELVED IN MY MOTHER'S HUTCH, BUT THE *CHAWAN MUSHI*, WHICH CLASSICALLY INCLUDES CHICKEN AND/OR SHRIMP, HAS MIGRATED INTO MY VEGETARIAN REPERTOIRE.

If using fresh shiitakes, trim off the stems, wipe the caps, and set aside. If using dried shiitakes, place them in the dashi until soft, about 20 minutes. Remove, trim off the stems, and set the caps aside, reserving the dashi in a medium bowl.

Bring a small pot of water to boil. Drop the trefoil into the water and remove immediately. Set aside. In the same water, parboil the asparagus and carrot together until slightly soft, about 2 minutes. Drain and set aside.

Break the eggs into a medium bowl and beat lightly with a fork or chopsticks. Stir in the dashi, soy sauce, mirin, and salt, whisking gently so as not to aerate the eggs.

Divide the asparagus and carrot among 4 10-ounce custard cups. Ladle the egg mixture into the custard cups, up to ¼ inch from the tops. Place a shiitake cap in each cup.

Fill a steamer with water and bring to a boil. Set the cups in the steamer, cover, and cook over high heat for 5 minutes. Reduce the heat to medium and continue to cook for 15 minutes more, or until the custard is set but still jiggly. Or place the cups in a microwave oven, cover with a plate, and microwave on high for 11 minutes. Remove and let stand for 2 minutes.

Garnish each custard with the trefoil and serve hot.

---

4 small shiitake mushrooms, fresh or dried

3 cups *Vegetable Dashi* (page 37)

4 stems mitsuba (trefoil) (page 13) or scallion tops

4 asparagus tips, top 1½ inches only

½ small carrot, scraped and sliced into ⅛-inch thick ovals

4 large eggs

1 teaspoon soy sauce

1 teaspoon mirin

½ teaspoon sea salt

CHAPTER THREE

RICE

THE EMINENT GRAIN

TO PRODUCE A PERFECT BOWL OF RICE FOR THE JAPANESE TABLE, THE COOK MUST TURN OUT GRAINS SOFT ON THE OUTSIDE WITH A BIT OF CRUNCH IN THE CENTER, MUCH LIKE ITALIAN RISOTTO, BUT WITH THE GRAINS MORE INDIVIDUAL, LESS LIQUID BOUND. Such delicacy is accomplished by prewashing and soaking the grains before cooking to begin the softening process; the technique is followed whether the rice is for a plain bowl or a composed dish, and whether the rice is new or old, white or brown. In this chapter are the basics for cooking perfect rice the Japanese way, plus two easy dishes for using leftover rice and several classic-to-modern composed rice dishes.

BASIC STEAMED RICE

❀

SERVES 4 TO 6

THE RIGHT POT IS IMPORTANT FOR RICE COOKING. MANY JAPANESE COOKS THESE DAYS RELY ON THE NEARLY INFALLIBLE RICE COOKER, BUT IF YOU DON'T HAVE ONE, CHOOSE A HEAVY POT WITH A WELL-FITTED LID LARGE ENOUGH TO HOLD THE RICE AND WATER REACHING HALF AN INCH ABOVE THE GRAINS AT THE BEGINNING OF COOKING. THE FOLLOWING RECIPE IS ENOUGH TO SERVE FOUR IF THE RICE IS TO BE THE BASIS OF A COMPOSED DISH OR SIX IF THE RICE IS TO BE A SIDE DISH. IF YOU ARE COOKING MORE OR LESS, ADJUST THE POT SIZE TO ACCOMMODATE THE RICE AND WATER AS DESCRIBED.

Place the rice in a medium-sized heavy pot. Add plenty of water, swish the rice, and drain. Repeat the process 2 more times, until the water is nearly clear, no longer cloudy. Drain the rice, return it to the pot and add 2 cups fresh water. Set aside to soak for at least 30 minutes or up to 1 hour.

Bring the rice and its soaking water to a boil over medium-high heat. Adjust the heat to maintain a very gentle simmer, cover the pot, and cook for 13 minutes. Without lifting the lid, turn off the heat and leave the pot on the burner to finish steaming and drying for at least twenty minutes. Thirty minutes is better, and up to 1 hour is fine for still warm rice.

With a wooden spoon or rice paddle, gently lift and toss the grains to fluff them. Serve right away or proceed with another recipe for a composed rice dish.

1½ cups short-grain rice

NEW RICE

RICE IS NEW IN AUTUMN. FROM THEN UNTIL NEW YEAR'S, THE TENDER GRAINS ARE APPRECIATED FOR THEIR INHERENT SWEETNESS, SOFTNESS, AND PRECIOUS, PEARL-LIKE APPEARANCE. NEW RICE IS SELDOM EXPANDED UPON OR COLORED WITH ANY OTHER INGREDIENT. PLAIN IS TRULY BEST HERE. IF YOU HAVE THE GOOD FORTUNE TO RECEIVE A HANDFUL OR TWO OF NEW RICE, COOK IT AS YOU WOULD BASIC STEAMED RICE, BUT ADJUST THE WATER SO THAT THE RATIO OF RICE TO WATER IS 1:1, AND REDUCE THE COOKING TIME TO A MERE TEN MINUTES.

BROWN RICE

SERVES 4 TO 6

FROM TEMPLE HIERARCHS TO HUMBLE LABORERS TO CITY DWELLERS, JAPANESE GENERALLY PREFER WHITE RICE. THERE IS, HOWEVER, A SUBCULTURE TRADITION BASED ON A VEGETARIAN MACROBIOTIC DIET THAT ALWAYS CALLS FOR BROWN RICE. IT'S THOUGHT THAT SINCE BROWN RICE IS UNHULLED IT RETAINS THE VITAMINS AND MINERALS THAT ARE WASHED AWAY IN THE PROCESSING OF WHITE RICE. FOR MYSELF, I OFTEN CHOOSE BROWN RICE FOR ITS NUTTIER FLAVOR AND MORE RUSTIC TEXTURE. THE BASIC TECHNIQUE FOR PREPARING AND COOKING BROWN RICE IS THE SAME AS THAT FOR WHITE, EXCEPT THE COOKING TIME IS LONGER.

Wash the rice as described on page 53. Drain the grains, put them in the cooking pot, and add 3 cups fresh water. Set aside to soak for at least 30 minutes or up to 1 hour.

Bring the rice and its soaking water to a boil over medium-high heat. Adjust the heat to maintain a gentle simmer, cover the pot, and cook for 40 minutes. Without lifting the lid, turn off the heat and leave the pot on the burner to finish steaming and drying for at least 20 minutes. Fluff the rice and serve right away or use for another dish.

1½ cups short-grain brown rice

LEFTOVER RICE

GENEROUS COOKS, FAMILY COOKS ESPECIALLY, ALWAYS MAKE SURE TO PREPARE ENOUGH RICE SO THERE IS A LITTLE EXTRA FOR A SNACK LATER, FOR SCHOOL LUNCH TOMORROW, OR FOR AN EARLY MORNING EAT-AND-RUN PREPARATION. LEFTOVER RICE SHOULD BE COVERED AND SET ASIDE AT ROOM TEMPERATURE, NOT REFRIGERATED. IT WILL KEEP FOR UP TO TWO DAYS. CHILLING RICE CAUSES THE GRAINS TO HARDEN AND LOSE MUCH OF THEIR SWEETNESS. ◆ TO REHEAT LEFTOVER RICE, PLACE IT IN A MICROWAVE BOWL, SPRINKLE WITH WATER, COVER, AND MICROWAVE ON HIGH FOR 2 TO 3 MINUTES, DEPENDING ON THE AMOUNT. OR ON THE STOVETOP, SPRINKLE THE RICE WITH WATER, COVER, AND SET THE POT OVER AS LOW AS POSSIBLE HEAT FOR 5 TO 10 MINUTES, DEPENDING ON THE AMOUNT, UNTIL STEAMING AGAIN.

RICE BALLS WITH PICKLED PLUMS AND GREEN SHISO

❁

MAKES 6 RICE BALLS

RICE BALLS, OR SOMETIMES RICE TRIANGLES OR RICE CYLINDERS, ARE THE DAILY WAY TO USE LEFTOVER RICE. A SALTY ORANGE-RED PICKLED PLUM, THE ONE CALLED UMEBOSHI, TUCKED IN THE CENTER TRANSFORMS THE ORDINARY FARE INTO A SPECIAL TREAT. THE FRESH AND AROMATIC GREEN SHISO LEAF COVERING, IN PLACE OF THE TRADITIONAL NORI SEAWEED WRAP, RENDERS THE TREAT SUBLIME. YOU CAN SUBSTITUTE ONE OR TWO DRIED CRANBERRIES SOFTENED IN SAKE TO PROVIDE THE RED COLOR AND TARTNESS OF THE UMEBOSHI, BUT YOU'LL MISS OUT ON ITS FRUITY SALTINESS. TO FORM RICE BALLS, HAVE THE RICE WARM AND SHAPE IT WITH WET HANDS; OTHERWISE, THE RICE WILL STICK TO YOUR FINGERS.

With wet hands form ¼-cup amounts of the rice into 6 balls or triangles. Push a plum into the center of each and squeeze firmly to enclose the plum. Arrange the balls on a serving plate and set aside.

Rinse the shiso leaves in warm water to wilt slightly and spread a leaf on top of each rice ball. Serve right away, or refrigerate for up to 2 hours and serve chilled.

1½ cups Basic Steamed Rice (see page 53), warm or reheated

6 umeboshi (pickled plums), pitted

6 green shiso (perilla) leaves

SESAME·CRUSTED RICE PATTIES

MAKES 6 PATTIES

IF YOU'RE ONE WHO CAN'T RESIST A POTATO LATKE, YOU MIGHT FIND YOURSELF MAKING LOTS OF RICE, TO HAVE LEFTOVERS AND TURN THE COOKED RICE INTO THESE SESAME-CRUSTED PATTIES. THE UNORTHODOX, BUT NOT UNHEARD OF, WHEAT FLOUR BINDING, AS IN LATKES, PROVIDES ESSENTIAL FLAVOR AS WELL AS COHESION FOR THE RICE GRAINS.

1½ cups Basic Steamed Rice (see page 53), warm or reheated
1 tablespoon flour
½ teaspoon sea salt
1 large or 2 small scallions, trimmed and minced
1 tablespoon sesame seeds, preferably black
Vegetable oil, for frying

Place the rice, flour, salt, and scallions in a medium bowl. With wet hands, mix until well blended. Form the mixture into 6 patties, rewetting your hands as you go to keep the rice from sticking. Sprinkle both sides of the patties with sesame seeds, set them on a plate, and let rest at room temperature for 1 hour.

When ready to cook, pour a small amount of oil, more than enough to coat the pan but not so much as to float the patties, into a frying pan and heat until beginning to smoke. Place as many patties as will fit in a single uncrowded layer in the pan. Fry over medium-high heat until lightly golden, about 1 minute. Turn and fry until golden on the other side, about 1 minute more. Transfer to a platter and continue until all the patties are fried. Serve right away.

RICE WITH ROLLED OMELET RIBBONS

☙

SERVES 4

WHILE THE JAPANESE ARE ADAMANT ABOUT SOUP AND BROTHY NOODLE DISHES BEING SERVED PIPING HOT, MANY OF THE RICE DISHES FOR FAMILY MEALS ARE SERVED AT ROOM TEMPERATURE. FOR THIS AND OTHER STEAMED RICE DISHES, YOU CAN PREPARE THE RICE, SET IT ASIDE, TO STAY WARM, AND PADDLE IN THE ADDED INGREDIENTS JUST BEFORE SERVING. ◆ INSTRUCTIONS FOR THE JAPANESE-STYLE OMELET MAY SEEM COMPLICATED, BUT ACTUALLY IT'S JUST A MATTER OF QUICKLY SEARING PART OF THE EGG MIXTURE, FOLDING IT ASIDE, AND CONTINUING UNTIL YOU HAVE THREE LAYERS. A BAMBOO ROLLING MAT IS A BOON FOR THE ROLLING PART. BUT YOU CAN USE A CLOTH OR STURDY PAPER TOWEL INSTEAD.

1 cup watercress sprigs, thick stems
    removed, or 12 stems
    mitsuba (trefoil)
2 carrots, peeled and cut diagonally into
    thin ovals
1 recipe Basic Steamed Rice (page 53),
    warm or reheated

Rolled Omelet

3 large eggs
2 teaspoons sake
¼ teaspoon sugar
⅛ teaspoon sea salt
Vegetable oil, for frying

Bring a small pot of lightly salted water to boil. Drop in the watercress sprigs and remove them immediately with a slotted spoon. Set aside. Add the carrots to the water and boil for 1 minute, or until the carrots are barely wilted. Drain and set aside. Gently mix the carrots into the warm rice.

To make the omelet, whisk together the eggs, sake, sugar, and salt without frothing the eggs. Coat an omelet pan with oil and wipe with a paper towel so that the pan is very lightly coated. Set the pan over medium-high heat until smoking. Pour a third of the egg mixture into the pan, and tilt to coat with egg mixture all the way up the sides. With chopsticks or a wooden spoon, lift one edge of the egg mixture and fold it over twice, away from you, toward the back of the pan, to make a roll.

Re-oil the front of the pan, move the egg roll forward, and re-oil the back of the pan. Pour half of the remaining egg mixture into the pan, tilt the pan to coat again, and lift the already-cooked egg roll so that the new mixture flows underneath it. Roll up the egg mixture, this time enclosing the first roll within the second. Repeat the process with the last third of the egg mixture. Gently lift the final egg roll out of the pan and transfer to a rolling mat, setting the egg roll at the edge of the mat. Roll up the mat, enclosing the egg roll, and press down gently. Let rest for 10 minutes before cutting.

Slice the omelet roll crosswise into ⅛-inch-wide sections. Pull the slices apart into ribbons and strew the ribbons over the top of the rice. Arrange the watercress to make a decorative dish and serve.

RICE AND RED BEANS WITH OKRA

❀

SERVES 4 TO 6

RICE AND RED BEANS, ESPECIALLY WITH OKRA, MAY CONJURE IMAGES OF SULTRY SOUTHERN DAYS OR JAZZ NIGHTS IN NEW ORLEANS'S OLD QUARTER. IT COULD EQUALLY WELL BRING TO MIND A FESTIVE OCCASION IN JAPAN WHERE AN OFFERING OF RED RICE, COLORED BY AZUKI BEANS, SIGNIFIES THE HAPPY NATURE OF THE EVENT. A SPRINKLING OF BLACK SESAME SEEDS CUSTOMARILY FINISHES THE DISH, BUT IN A PAN-PACIFIC SIDESTEP HERE, OKRA, A FAVORED JAPANESE VEGETABLE, PROVIDES A SPARK OF GREEN INSTEAD AND MAKES FOR A MEAL IN A BOWL.

12 medium (4 to 6 ounces) okra pods,
    stems trimmed off
½ teaspoon sea salt
2 teaspoons rice vinegar
1 recipe Basic Steamed Rice (see page
    53), warm or reheated
¾ cup cooked red beans (see page 119)
Shichimi (see page 14), or red chili
    flakes, to taste

Place the okra in a bowl, add the salt and vinegar, and toss to mix. Set aside for at least 30 minutes or up to 1 hour.

Bring a medium pot of water to a boil. Slice the okra pods diagonally into 1-inch pieces and add to the water. Cook over high heat for 1 minute, or until wilted but still bright green. Drain and set aside.

Mound the rice on a serving platter or in individual bowls. Place some okra on top and some red beans alongside. Sprinkle shichimi over the top and serve.

NEW YEAR'S RICE WITH CHESTNUTS AND MIZUNA

SERVES 4 TO 6

WHEREVER THEY GROW, CHESTNUTS ANNOUNCE THE ARRIVAL OF FALL, COLD WEATHER, AND DIMINISHING LIGHT. IN JAPAN, THE MEALY MORSELS ARE SIMMERED IN SAVORY SIDE DISHES, PUREED FOR DESSERT, AND, IN A HALCYON OFFERING, MIXED INTO RICE TO INSURE PROSPERITY FOR THE NEW YEAR. IT'S AN UNUSUAL PREPARATION IN THAT THE RICE IS FLAVORED WITH SALT AND SAKE AND THE CHESTNUTS ARE ADDED DURING COOKING RATHER THAN PADDLED IN AFTER THE RICE IS STEAMED. CUSTOMARILY THE RICE IS WHITE; HERE, IT'S BROWN BECAUSE I LIKE THE DOUBLE NUTTINESS PROVIDED BY BROWN RICE. FOR CHROMATIC RELIEF, I STREW WILTED MIZUNA OVER THE TOP.

To prepare the chestnuts, make a slit in the top of each with a paring knife. Bring a small pot of water to a boil and drop in the chestnuts. Boil for 6 minutes, then remove the pot from the heat without draining. As soon as the chestnuts are cool enough to handle, remove one from the liquid, leaving the rest to soak. With a paring knife and your fingers, peel and skin it. Continue until all the chestnuts are peeled. Halve any that are still whole. Set aside at room temperature or refrigerate until ready to use. (Chestnuts may be refrigerated for up to 5 days.)

Drain the rice and place in a medium pot along with 3 cups of water, the sake, salt, and chestnuts. Bring to a boil, cover, and simmer over very low heat for 40 minutes. Turn off the heat and leave the rice on the burner, without lifting the lid, for 20 minutes.

While the rice cooks, bring a small pot of water to boil. Stir in the mizuna, drain immediately, and rinse with cool water. Press out excess moisture, and set aside.

When the rice is ready, spread the mizuna over the top and serve.

NOTE: To save time you can purchase canned chestnuts, already prepared. These suffice for flavor but lack the firm texture ideal for this preparation. The best alternative is to purchase whole peeled chestnuts, steamed and vacuum-packed either in jars or plastic wrap, which you can occasionally find in gourmet food shops. They're quite pricy, but perhaps worth it for a prosperity dish.

12 to 18 fresh chestnuts (see Note)

1½ cups short-grain brown rice, well rinsed and soaked for 30 minutes

3 tablespoons sake

½ teaspoon sea salt

1 cup (packed) coarsely chopped mizuna leaves

SUSHI BASICS

✿

ALL THE WORLD LOVES SUSHI, AND IT'S EASY TO SEE WHY. SUSHI IS AN INGENIOUS WAY WITH RICE. IF YOU'VE EVER SAT AT A SUSHI BAR, CAPTIVATED BY THE SIGHT OF THE HANDS OF THE *ITAMAE* (SUSHI MASTER) DEFTLY, QUICKLY TURNING OUT JEWEL AFTER DELECTABLE JEWEL, YOU CAN UNDERSTAND THE ENCHANTMENT. ON THE OTHER HAND, THE PROCESS APPEARS SO MAGICAL AND THE POSSIBILITIES SO NUMEROUS, IT SEEMS DAUNTING, A CRAFT FOR MASTERS. NOT SO. THERE IS A LOGIC TO SUSHI MAKING, AND WHILE THE ART IS UP TO THE COOK, THE CRAFT IS ACCESSIBLE IN FIVE BASIC FORMS. ◆ IN THIS SECTION, YOU WILL FIND A SELECTION OF NORI-WRAPPED VEGETARIAN SUSHIS THAT RANGE FROM THE STANDARD KAPPA MAKI TO THE INNOVATIVE INSIDE-OUT NORI ROLL; A FANCIFUL *TEMAKI*-SUSHI, HAND-ROLL PARTY TRAY; AND *CHIRASI*-SUSHI, SO POPULAR WITH HOME COOKS. I ALSO INCLUDE *INARI*-SUSHI IN CASE YOU HAVE TOFU PUFFS (*ABURAGE*) AND WOULD LIKE TO SOLVE THE ONGOING WHAT'S-FOR-SCHOOL-LUNCH-TODAY PROBLEM IN A DELIGHTFUL NEW WAY.

NIGIRI-SUSHI: Ovals or rounds of sushi rice with thinly sliced raw fish on top; a prized version of sushi. Nigiri-sushi is not included in this book.

MAKI-SUSHI: Nori seaweed wrapped around sushi rice with vegetable and/or fish bits inside.

TEMAKI-SUSHI: Nori seaweed squares or rectangles with sushi rice and vegetable and/or fish bits loosely rolled into a cone. Called hand-roll sushi because the elements are often presented on a party buffet platter for guests to assemble as desired with their own hands.

INARI-SUSHI: Simmered tofu puffs (*aburage*) filled with sushi rice, sometimes including sesame seeds and/or tiny bits of diced vegetable.

CHIRASHI-SUSHI: The sushi rice is presented in a bowl with its additions topped on, not rolled at all. Called scattered sushi, it's a family dish for making a meal out of sushi rice, popular with home cooks.

✿

EQUIPMENT AND INGREDIENT NEEDS

A BAMBOO ROLLING MAT: Called a *makisu*, it is essential for ease of making *maki*-sushi. With a mat, you can roll away to your heart's content. It's also a most useful household object that can double as a trivet for warm pots or decorative mat for flower vases. Bamboo rolling mats are to be found in Japanese markets, hardware stores, and sometimes supermarkets serving a multinational clientele.

A BOWL OF LIGHTLY VINEGARED WATER: To keep your hands moist and clean as you roll the sushi.

ROASTED NORI SEAWEED: Nori sheets are ready to fill and roll; no further preparation is required. Each sheet has a shiny side and a slightly nubby side. Sushi is rolled with the shiny side out, so place the sheet nubby side up when assembling the ingredients. The recipes in this section are for eight sheets. The extra two sheets in the package may be shredded and used to garnish other Japanese dishes (use a scissors to cut the nori) or enjoyed as a snack—children and cats find nori quite a treat.

BASIC TECHNIQUE FOR NORI-WRAPPED SUSHI

1. Lay the bamboo mat on the counter.

2. Place a nori sheet, nubby side up, on top of the mat.

3. With wet hands, spread a thin layer of sushi rice over the nori, covering it to within ¼ inch of the edges.

4. Arrange the ingredients you are using in the center of the rice layer.

5. Using the mat as a guide, roll up the nori, rice, and filling into a tight roll, without including the mat inside the roll!

6. Lightly press down on the roll to compress the ingredients, then remove the bamboo mat.

7. Cut the roll crosswise into 8 sections. Place each section, face up, on a plate and serve.

SUSHI RICE

❀

MAKES ABOUT 7 CUPS, ENOUGH FOR 8 SUSHI ROLLS

SUSHI RICE DIFFERS LITTLE FROM REGULAR JAPANESE-STYLE RICE, EXCEPT THAT ONCE STEAMED, THE GRAINS ARE TOSSED WITH SWEETENED RICE VINEGAR. IT'S ALSO IMPORTANT TO FAN THE GRAINS WHILE MIXING TO COOL THEM AND BRING OUT THEIR GLOSS. AN EXTRA PAIR HANDS HELPS, BUT THE LONE COOK CAN MANAGE BY WORKING RAPIDLY, ALTERNATELY FANNING AND MIXING. THE OPTIONAL KELP MAKES THE DIFFERENCE BETWEEN OK AND TRULY AUTHENTIC-TASTING SUSHI RICE.

2 cups short-grain rice

2-inch piece kombu kelp (optional)

¼ cup rice vinegar

1½ to 2 tablespoons sugar (see Notes)

1 teaspoon sea salt

Place the rice in a medium bowl and rinse well. Drain and set aside for 1 hour.

Place the rice and 2½ cups water in a medium-sized heavy saucepan. Wipe the kelp, if using, with a damp cloth and add to the pot. Bring to a boil over medium-high heat, immediately remove the kelp, and reserve it for another dish.

Adjust the heat so the rice simmers very gently, cover the pot, and cook for 20 minutes. Turn off the heat and let the pot rest on the burner for 20 minutes without lifting the lid.

While the rice cooks, stir together the vinegar, sugar, and salt in a small non-reactive saucepan or microwave bowl. Heat the mixture until it begins to boil and stir again to dissolve the sugar. Set aside to cool until ready to use.

When the rice has rested, transfer it to a wooden or glass bowl. With a wooden spoon or paddle, very gently mix it a bit to separate the grains. Pour the vinegar mixture over the rice and continue mixing until all the grains are coated. At the same time, use a newspaper or other fan to cool the grains as you mix. Set aside at room temperature for up to several hours until ready to use.

NOTES: For sushi rice, all like it sweetened; some like it very sweet. The lesser amount of sugar called for is to my taste.

If making in advance, regulate the timing so that you can use the rice and serve the sushi the same day without refrigerating, which hardens the rice and diminishes the sweetness of the sushi.

SUSHI HAND ROLL

SERVES 8 TO 12

HAND-ROLL SUSHI, OR *TEMAKI*-SUSHI, IS A CONSUMMATE PARTY DISH. THE HOST OR HOSTESS CAN LAY OUT THE INGREDIENTS AND PRESENT THEM WITH A BOWL OF SUSHI RICE AND A BASKET OF ROASTED NORI SQUARES. ALL THAT'S LEFT IS TO LET THE GUESTS HAVE AT IT WHILE SCHMOOZING AND OBSERVING HOW EACH ONE APPROACHES THE TRAY AND WRAPS A PERSONAL BITE. THE INGREDIENT LIST BELOW IS MEANT TO BE SUGGESTIVE; SIX CHOICES, ALONG WITH THE CONDIMENTS, MORE THAN SUFFICE FOR A GALA PRESENTATION.

Whisk together the wasabi powder and 6 tablespoons water in a small bowl. Put the ginger, daikon, soy sauce, and wasabi paste in separate bowls and place on the table. Set aside.

Arrange as many of the ingredients as you are using on a large tray. Place on the table. Using scissors, cut the nori into half or quarter sheets and arrange them in a basket or on a plate. Place on the table.

Place the rice in a serving bowl, set on the table, and invite the guests to wrap and enjoy as they please.

Condiments

1 recipe Pickled Ginger (page 24)

1 recipe Shredded Daikon (page 70)

Soy sauce

½ cup wasabi powder

Ingredients Tray

1 cucumber, slivered

1 Burdock Root Simmered with Sake (page 93)

4 strips kampyo, softened and simmered for sushi (see page 12)

3 ounces daikon or other sprouts

4 scallions, trimmed and shredded

6 green shiso (perilla) leaves, shredded

6 umeboshi (pickled plums), halved and pitted

1 Rolled Omelet (page 60), sliced crosswise into ¼-inch-wide strips

1 ripe but still firm avocado, peeled, pitted, and thinly sliced

8 sheets roasted nori

1 recipe Sushi Rice (page 66)

CUCUMBER ROLL WITH SHREDDED DAIKON GARNISH

NORI-WRAPPED, CUCUMBER-FILLED *KAPPA-MAKI* SUSHI MAINTAINS A STATUS AS THE BUTLER OF SUSHI EATING. CALMLY IT USHERS YOU IN AND COOLLY INVITES YOU TO BEGIN THE SUSHI DINING ADVENTURE. STILL, IN SPITE OF ITS QUIET NORMALCY, *KAPPA-MAKI* CONTAINS A SURPRISE: THE WASABI BITE IN THE CENTER OF THE ROLL IS SINGULAR AMONG THE *MAKI-SUSHIS* WHICH USUALLY DO NOT INCLUDE IT. ◆ THE NEST OF EVER SO FINELY SHREDDED DAIKON THAT APPEARS AS A GARNISH WITH THIS AND MANY OTHER JAPANESE DISHES INVOLVES CUTTING THE DAIKON INTO THIN SHEETS, THEN STACKING THE SHEETS AND SLICING THEM INTO THREADS. THE HOME COOK CAN USE A FOOD PROCESSOR, WHICH DOES A FINE JOB OF JULIENNING, THOUGH NOT SO REFINED. THE BEAUTY OF THE CUT AND NATURAL PIQUANCY OF THE DAIKON NEED NO FURTHER SEASONING.

2 tablespoons wasabi powder

8 sheets roasted nori

1 recipe Sushi Rice (page 66)

1 cucumber, preferably Japanese, trimmed
  and cut into thin slivers

Shredded Daikon (recipe follows)

Soy sauce, for serving

Whisk together the wasabi powder and 1½ tablespoons water in a small bowl. Set aside for 5 minutes.

Place 1 sheet of nori on a bamboo mat and cover with sushi rice as described on page 65. Spread a film of wasabi along the center of the rice, arrange cucumber slivers over the wasabi, and roll up. Continue until all the sheets are rolled. Cut and arrange the pieces on a serving platter or individual plates. Garnish with the daikon and serve with soy sauce on the side.

SHREDDED DAIKON

2-inch piece daikon

Peel the daikon. Cut it lengthwise as thin as possible. Stack the slices into manageable piles and cut again lengthwise as thin as possible into shreds. Use as a garnish for sushi or salads. (Shredded daikon will keep for up to 1 day in the refrigerator.)

INSIDE·OUT SUSHI ROLL

✦

INSIDE-OUT *MAKI*-SUSHI IS THE NEW KID ON THE BLOCK AS FAR AS SUSHI ROLLS GO. INSPIRED BY THE POPULAR CALIFORNIA ROLL THAT FEATURES AVOCADO, ALSO AN EXCELLENT SUSHI INGREDIENT THAT MARRIES WELL WITH RICE AND SPICE, THIS ONE FOLLOWS THE TASTE AND TECHNIQUE WITHOUT INCLUDING THE CUSTOMARY CRAB AND SUBSTITUTES SLICED RED VEGETABLES IN PLACE OF TOBIKO ROE TO DUST THE OUTSIDE OF THE ROLL.

Spread the sesame seeds in a small dry skillet or on a microwave plate. Stir over medium-high heat or microwave on high for 3 minutes, or until lightly toasted. Set aside.

Whisk together the wasabi powder and 1½ tablespoons water in a small bowl. Set aside for 5 minutes.

Place 1 sheet of nori on a bamboo mat and cover with sushi rice as described on page 65. Lift the nori off the mat, turn it over onto the mat so that the rice is now on the bottom and the nori on top. Spread a film of wasabi along the center of the nori. Arrange cucumber and avocado strips over the wasabi. With wet hands, and without using the mat, roll up as neatly as possible.

Cover the roll with a sheet of plastic wrap and set on the bamboo mat again. This time using the mat, roll up tightly. Remove the mat and the plastic wrap. Finally, sprinkle the outside of the roll with sesame seeds and minced bell pepper or carrot. Set aside and continue until all the rolls are formed. Slice the rolls crosswise into 6 pieces. Arrange the pieces face side up on a platter or individual plates and serve.

1½ teaspoons white sesame seeds

2 tablespoons wasabi powder

8 sheets roasted nori seaweed

1 recipe Sushi Rice (page 66)

1 cucumber, preferably Japanese, trimmed and cut into thin slivers

1 ripe but still firm avocado, peeled, pitted, and thinly sliced lengthwise

⅓ cup finely minced red bell pepper or carrot, blanched, drained, and patted dry

KAMPYO AND ONION SPROUT SUSHI

✿

MAKES 8 ROLLS, 48 PIECES

SUSHI CHEFS FROM TOKYO TO SAN FRANCISCO, LOS ANGELES, NEW YORK, AND PARIS CREATE FANCIFUL SUSHI ROLLS TO ENTERTAIN THEIR PATRONS—AND THEMSELVES, TOO, I SUSPECT. HOME COOKS CAN DO THE SAME. THIS ONE IS MY FUN. THERE'S NO SUBSTITUTE FOR THE KAMPYO EXCEPT FOR ANOTHER IDEA OF YOUR OWN.

8 sheets roasted nori seaweed

1 recipe Sushi Rice (page 66)

4 strands kampyo, softened and
  simmered for sushi (see page 12)

2 to 3 ounces onion sprouts (see Note)

1 tablespoon finely chopped lemon zest

Soy sauce, for serving

Place 1 sheet of nori on a bamboo mat and cover with rice as described on page 00. Arrange strips of kampyo and sprouts along the center of the rice, sprinkle with lemon zest, and roll up. Continue until all the sheets are rolled. Cut and arrange the slices on a plate and serve with soy sauce on the side.

NOTE: In place of onion sprouts, substitute daikon, radish, or any other piquant, nippy sprout.

SCATTERED SUSHI

✤

SERVES 4

A COLLECTION OF SUSHI RECIPES WOULD NOT BE COMPLETE WITHOUT AN ENTRY FOR SCATTERED SUSHI. NOTHING FANCY ABOUT IT, SCATTERED SUSHI IS A FAMILY DISH FOR MAKING A MEAL OUT OF SUSHI RICE WITHOUT THE CHORE OF FILLING, ROLLING, AND SLICING NORI SHEETS FOR INDIVIDUAL BITES. AS IT IS A HOME-STYLE DISH, THE INGREDIENTS INCLUDED DEPEND AS MUCH ON WHAT IS AT HAND AS ON A PRESCRIBED LIST OF "MUST-HAVES." FOLLOWING IS MY PARTICULAR FAVORITE COMBINATION.

Bring 2 cups of water to a boil in a medium saucepan. Add the green beans and blanch until softened but still bright green and crunchy, about 3 minutes. With a slotted spoon, remove the beans to a colander, reserving the water, and set aside.

If using shiitake mushrooms, cut off the stems. Wipe the mushrooms and cut them into ¼-inch thick slices.

Add the soy sauce and mirin to the reserved water. Add the mushrooms, leek, and tofu puff, if using. Bring to a boil, then simmer until the vegetables are well wilted but not soft, about 5 minutes. Add the carrots and continue simmering until the carrots are cooked but still crisp, about 5 minutes. Remove the pot from the heat and set aside without draining the vegetables.

Stir together the eggs, sugar, and salt in a small bowl, whisking to mix well without aerating the eggs. Lightly coat a medium skillet or omelet pan with oil and heat until beginning to smoke. Pour half the egg mixture into the pan and tilt the pan so that the mixture thinly covers the whole bottom. Cook over medium-high heat until the egg is no longer moist but not crisped, about 1 minute. Transfer the omelet to a large plate and cook the remaining egg mixture in the same way. Cut the omelets into thin strips.

To assemble the sushi, divide the rice among 4 large, dinner-sized bowls. Using a slotted spoon, lift the vegetables out of the liquid in the pot and scatter them over the rice. Sprinkle the green beans over the top and mound the omelet strips in the center. Garnish with a large pinch of ginger and serve.

VARIATIONS: Snow or snap peas, julienned and blanched; lotus root, peeled, thinly sliced, and simmered; Shredded Daikon (page 70) for garnish; roasted nori, slivered and sprinkled over the top.

4 ounces green beans, trimmed and sliced into thin rounds or ovals

3 medium fresh shiitake mushrooms or an equal amount of other wild mushrooms, such as chanterelle, tree ear, or oyster mushrooms

1 small leek, trimmed well washed, and sliced into thin rounds

1 tofu puff (aburage), rinsed in boiling water and cut crosswise into thin strips (optional)

1 carrot, scraped and cut into julienne strips or thin rounds

1 tablespoon soy sauce

2 tablespoons mirin

2 large eggs

¼ teaspoon sugar

Pinch of sea salt

Vegetable oil, for coating skillet

1 recipe Sushi Rice (page 66)

Pickled Ginger (page 24), for garnish

MOON·VIEWING NOODLES WITH SOFT·COOKED QUAIL EGGS

❧

SERVES 4 TO 6

A LATE SUMMER TO AUTUMN DISH, WHEN THE MOON IS PARTICULARLY VISIBLE IN CLEAR, CRISP SKIES, MOON-VIEWING NOODLES INVITE YOU TO SUP AND BE CALM WHILE ENJOYING THE HEAVENLY VIEW. BOTH SOBA AND UDON NOODLES ARE TRADITIONALLY USED; EITHER SUITS TO BOLSTER THE BRISK AND BUSY COLD DAYS TO COME.

If using udon noodles, cook and soak them according to the directions on page 78. Just before serving, bring a large pot of water to a boil. Drain the noodles, drop them into the boiling water just long enough to reheat, and drain again. If using soba noodles cook and drain them according to the directions on page 79, just before serving so they stay warm.

Place the spinach in a medium nonreactive pot or microwave bowl and heat until wilted but still bright green, about 2 minutes. Set aside.

Stir together the dashi and ginger and heat in a nonreactive pot or microwave bowl.

Divide the noodles among individual serving bowls. Moisten each with some of the dashi mixture. Place some of the spinach to the side of the noodles in each bowl and garnish with the egg halves. Serve right away, while still warm.

8 to 12 ounces dried udon or soba noodles
1½ cups tender spinach leaves, finely shredded, washed, and drained
4 cups warm Vegetable Dashi (page 37)
½ tablespoon grated fresh ginger
8 Soft-Cooked Quail Eggs (recipe follows), cut in half

SOFT·COOKED QUAIL EGGS

❧

Bring a small pot of water to a boil. With a spoon, gently place the eggs in the water and turn off the heat. Cover the pot and leave on the burner for 2 minutes. The whites will be set and the yolks still a little runny. For harder yolks, add 1 minute standing time. Drain, rinse under cool water until no longer warm, and set aside. Peel when ready to use.

8 quail eggs

SUMMER NOODLES

◈

SERVES 4

FROM JUNE TO AUGUST, EVERYWHERE IN JAPAN SOBA OR SOMEN NOODLES ARE EATEN COLD. SO PERVASIVE IS THE CUSTOM, THE DISH IS SIMPLY CALLED SUMMER NOODLES. AT THE JAPANESE TABLE, THE NOODLES, CONDIMENTS, AND FLAVORING SAUCE ARE SERVED SEPARATELY SO THAT EACH PERSON MAY DOLLOP AND MIX ACCORDING TO PERSONAL PREFERENCE. THE BASIC SET OF THREE CONDIMENTS— GINGER, SCALLION, AND WASABI—ARE PRETTY MUCH DE RIGUEUR. A MORE EXPANSIVE PRESENTATION MIGHT INCLUDE A PLATE OF THINLY SLICED SHIITAKES SIMMERED IN SEASONED DASHI, FINELY SHRED-DED JAPANESE EGG OMELET, FINELY SHREDDED ROASTED NORI, AND GRATED DAIKON OR CARROT.

2 tablespoons wasabi powder

1 tablespoon soy sauce

2 cups Vegetable Dashi (page 37)

1 tablespoon grated fresh ginger

¼ cup minced scallions

8 to 12 ounces soba or somen noodles,
   cooked and chilled

Whisk together the wasabi powder and 1½ tablespoons water in a small bowl. Set aside for 5 minutes.

Stir the soy sauce into the dashi and set on the table. Set out separate dishes containing the wasabi paste, ginger, and scallions. Divide the noodles among four bowls and serve, surrounded by the condiments already on the table.

SPRING NOODLES WITH TURNIP GREENS AND OYSTER MUSHROOMS

SERVES 4

DELICATE AND SOFT SOMEN NOODLES INVITE SPRING PRODUCE. TOGETHER WITH TENDER TURNIP GREENS, NEWLY SPROUTED OYSTER MUSHROOMS, AND A CRUNCHY GARNISH OF WALNUTS, THE FLAVORS OF LAND AND SEA ARE BROUGHT TOGETHER IN A NOODLE BOWL, JAPANESE STYLE.

3 cups Vegetable or Kombu Kelp Dashi
  (pages 37 and 38)

1 tablespoon sake

2 teaspoons soy sauce

¼ teaspoon sea salt

2 ounces oyster mushrooms, cut into
  ½-inch slices (see Notes)

1 cup coarsely chopped turnip greens (see
  Notes)

8 ounces somen noodles, cooked and
  drained (see page 79)

12 Savory Sweet Walnuts (page 27)

Combine the dashi, sake, soy sauce, and salt in a medium saucepan and bring to a boil. Add the mushrooms and greens and simmer until the greens are well wilted, about 2 minutes.

Divide the noodles among 4 individual bowls. Ladle the hot broth and vegetables over the noodles and garnish each bowl with 3 walnut halves. Serve right away.

NOTES: You can substitute equally delicate fresh enoki mushrooms, though they don't echo of the sea as do the oyster mushrooms. Fresh shiitakes would lend a peppery flavor to the broth. In any case, rather than resort to dried mushrooms for this dish, choose another one of the exotic fresh mushrooms available in the market. Spring vegetable options in place of the greens include parboiled fiddlehead ferns, slivered snow peas, or fava beans.

CHAPTER FIVE

VEGETABLES

VEGETABLES FOR ALL SEASONS

TO SPICE UP OR TONE DOWN THE NATURAL FLAVORS, VEGETABLES FOR THE JAPANESE TABLE ARE FINISHED IN NUMEROUS WAYS: DRESSED WITH SALTY AND SWEET MISO CONCOCTIONS OR SOY MIXTURES; GARNISHED WITH STRIDENT FLAVORINGS SUCH AS GINGER, SCALLION, LEMON ZEST, OR SHICHIMI (SEE PAGE 14); OR SIMPLY SPRINKLED WITH A LEAF OR SPRIG THAT SIGNIFIES THE SEASON. Taken together, the traditional finishings and dressings comprise a veritable lexicon of ways to adorn cooked vegetables, whether braised, blanched, grilled, or simmered, East or West style.

VEGETABLES FOR NEW YEAR'S

AS EVERYWHERE, NEW YEAR'S IN JAPAN IS A TIME FOR CELEBRATION. THE ANTICIPATION OVER CLOSING OLD ACCOUNTS AND TAKING UP NEW BEGINNINGS OCCUPIES PEOPLE'S THOUGHTS AND ACTIVITIES FOR MANY DAYS BEFORE. SO DO THE PREPARATIONS FOR CELEBRATORY VICTUALS. IN JAPAN, A FAMILY BANQUET TABLE IS THE FOCUS OF MUCH OF THIS ACTIVITY. THE ROOT VEGETABLES THAT ARE THE STAPLES OF WINTER — BURDOCK, LOTUS, CARROT, AND TARO — PLAY A MAJOR PART. INCLUDED IN THE FOLLOWING SELECTION FOR THE NEW YEAR'S TABLE ARE THE ABSOLUTELY NECESSARY BURDOCK AND LOTUS ROOTS AND THE LESS USUAL CELERY RIBS, ALSO A WINTER VEGETABLE.

ASPARAGUS IN MUSTARD·MISO DRESSING

SERVES 4

ASPARAGUS ARRIVES IN SPRING AND LASTS THROUGH EARLY SUMMER, THAT'S ALL. IT'S SPECIAL, AND IT DESERVES A SPECIAL TREATMENT. THOUGH NOT A TRADITIONAL JAPANESE VEGETABLE, ASPARAGUS IS APPRECIATED IN JAPAN. IN THIS DISH, THE ASPARAGUS SHOWCASES A DRESSING OF MISO AND MUSTARD, CLASSIC FOR COOKED GREEN VEGETABLES.

Snap the bottom ends off the asparagus. Cut the tips off to 2 inches long and slice the stems into ¼-inch-thick rounds. Rinse and drain.

Bring a medium pot of water to a boil. Add the asparagus and cook for 2 minutes. Drain, rinse under cool water, and set aside in the drainer for a few minutes.

When ready to serve, separate out the asparagus tips and place them in the middle of a serving plate. Arrange the asparagus rounds around the tips in a way that looks nice. Pour the dressing over all.

1 pound asparagus
½ cup Mustard-Miso Dressing
  (recipe follows)

MUSTARD·MISO DRESSING

MAKES ½ CUP

Mix the hot powdered mustard with 1 teaspoon water in a sake cup or small dish. Set aside for 5 minutes for the flavor to open.

Combine the mustard paste, miso, and mirin with 2 tablespoons water and whisk to mix. Use right away or within a few hours.

1 teaspoon hot powdered mustard
¼ cup white miso
1 tablespoon mirin

VEGETABLE TEMPURA

◉

SERVES 4

BESIDES SUSHI AND SUKIYAKI, TEMPURA REIGNS AS THE FAVORITE EXPORT OF JAPANESE CUISINE TO AMERICA. AFTER ALL, WHO DOESN'T LIKE FRIED FOOD? FOR WHEN YOU FEEL LIKE INDULGING, HERE'S THE GAME PLAN: HAVE THE DIPPING SAUCE READY. PREPARE ALL THE VEGETABLES IN ADVANCE. MAKE THE BATTER AT THE LAST MOMENT, SINCE IT SHOULD STILL BE COLD FROM THE ICE WATER. MOST IMPORTANTLY, BE PREPARED TO ATTEND THE STOVE BECAUSE TEMPURA SHOULD BE SERVED UP QUICKLY AFTER COOKING (A PAIR OF EXTRA HANDS AND TWO BURNERS HELP). AND, DON'T WORRY ABOUT VARYING COOKING TIMES—WHICHEVER THE VEGETABLE, IT'S DONE WHEN THE BATTER IS DONE.

First, prepare the vegetables. Make sure they are patted dry and set them aside until ready to cook, up to several hours.

When ready to cook, pour oil to a depth of 1½ to 2 inches into a large wok or heavy skillet or saucepan at least 3½ inches deep so there is enough room to allow for the oil to bubble up without boiling over. Set over high heat.

While the oil heats, prepare the batter. Using chopsticks, stir together the egg and ice water in a medium bowl. Add the flour and stir enough to mix into a lumpy, not smooth, batter. Test the oil temperature by dropping in a tiny bit of batter. The oil is ready when the batter rises immediately to the top and is golden, not white.

Dip as many vegetables as will fit in the pot without crowding into the batter and turn to coat. Place the vegetables in the oil and cook over medium-high to high heat, adjusting the temperature as you go so the oil stays hot but does not smoke, until the batter coating is deeply golden but not browned. Transfer to paper towels and continue with another round until all the vegetables are cooked.

Arrange on a platter and serve right away, accompanied by a bowl of the dipping sauce for each person.

NOTE: It's important that the water for the batter be very cold. You can place it in the refrigerator to chill before using, or add ice cubes to the water, then pour off the called for amount.

A selection of vegetables (see page 100), enough to allow 8 pieces per person
Vegetable oil, for frying
Tempura Dipping Sauce (recipe follows)

Batter
1 large egg
1 cup ice water (see Note)
1 cup all-purpose flour

As so many vegetables lend themselves to deep-frying, feel free to roam the world of produce possibilities and choose what appeals to you. Following is a brief list of classic and neoclassic selections that appeal to me:

CLASSIC VEGETABLES

BELL PEPPER, stemmed, seeded, and cut into 1-inch-wide strips

CHILI PEPPER, preferably small, such as jalapeño, stemmed, seeded, and halved

LOTUS ROOT, peeled and cut into ⅛-inch-thick rounds

MUSHROOMS, preferably shiitakes, stems cut off, caps wiped and left whole if small, cut into ¾-inch-wide strips if large

ONION, peeled, cut in half, and sliced ¼-inch thick

GREEN SHISO (PERILLA) LEAVES, left whole, rinsed, and patted dry

SWEET POTATO, peeled and cut into ¼-inch-thick rounds

NEWLY TRADITIONAL VEGETABLES

CARROT, scraped and cut into 3-by-¼-inch ovals

EGGPLANT, caps trimmed off and eggplant cut into ½-inch rounds or 2-inch lengths, depending on the type of eggplant

GREEN BEANS, stem ends trimmed off, beans cut into 2-inch lengths

ZUCCHINI, trimmed and sliced lengthwise into 3-by-⅛-inch pieces

NEW FUN

BABY ARTICHOKE, tough outer leaves pulled off down to the light green heart, stems and tops cut off, hearts cut in half lengthwise, chokes removed if any

ASPARAGUS TIPS

FENNEL BULB, tops trimmed, bulb sliced lengthwise as thin as possible

LEMON, rinsed, ends removed, and cut into ¼-inch-thick rounds

SPINACH ROOTS (see page 112)

TEMPURA DIPPING SAUCE

❀

SERVES 4

1 cup Vegetable Dashi (page 37)

3 tablespoons soy sauce

3 tablespoons mirin

½ cup finely grated daikon

1 teaspoon finely grated fresh ginger

Combine the dashi, soy sauce, and mirin in a small pan or microwave bowl and heat until beginning to boil. Set aside in a warm place.

When ready to serve, divide the warm sauce among individual bowls. Put a mound of daikon in the center of each bowl, top each mound with a small dollop of ginger, and place on the table at each person's place.

SWEET SIMMERED KABOCHA SQUASH

KABOCHA DISTINGUISHES ITSELF FROM OTHER GOURD-TYPE WINTER SQUASHES WITH ITS NATURAL SWEETNESS AND FIRM TEXTURE THAT HOLDS UP THROUGH COOKING. IN THIS SIMPLE PREPARATION, THE SQUASH SHINES THROUGH, SHOWING HOW A HUMBLE DISH CAN BE LOVELY IN THE SOFT LIGHT OF A SIMPLE, CLEAR PRESENTATION.

Cut the squash in half (crosswise through the equator line is easier than lengthwise from top to bottom) and scoop out the seeds. Peel the halves, leaving a bit of peel for color. Cut the squash into 1-by-2-inch wedges.

Combine sugar, salt, soy sauce, and 2½ cups water in a saucepan large enough to hold the squash pieces in 1 layer. Bring to a boil and add the squash. Bring back to a boil, reduce the heat, and simmer until the squash is tender but not mushy, about 12 minutes. Using a slotted spoon, transfer the squash to a bowl and reserve the liquid in the pan. Set aside the squash and the liquid until cooled to room temperature.

Arrange the squash in a serving bowl, moisten with some of the liquid, and serve.

NOTE: You can substitute acorn or butternut squash for the kabocha. Daikon and turnip also take well to this treatment.

1 medium (about 1½ pounds) kabocha squash (see Note)

¼ cup sugar

¼ teaspoon sea salt

1 tablespoon soy sauce

OKRA AND CRISPY NOODLES IN TOFU SESAME DRESSING

OKRA, A MEMBER OF THE MALLOW FAMILY (*HIBISCUS ESCULENTUS*), ORIGINATED IN THE NILE VALLEY OF NORTH AFRICA. TODAY, IT IS A CULINARY VEGETABLE ON FIVE CONTINENTS. STILL, WIDESPREAD AS IT IS, IN THE WORLD OF VEGETABLES OKRA ALL TOO OFTEN BESPEAKS COUNTRY PLAINNESS. HERE, MARINATED IN SALT AND VINEGAR, BLANCHED, TOSSED WITH A TYPICAL JAPANESE DRESSING REMINISCENT OF MAYONNAISE, AND HEAPED ON A BED OF CRISPY NOODLES, OKRA TURNS OUT TO BE SURPRISINGLY SOPHISTICATED. ◆ USE THE PROTEIN-RICH AND UNCTUOUS YET EGG- AND (ALMOST) OIL-FREE TOFU SESAME DRESSING FOR ANY VEGETABLE OR AS A SANDWICH SPREAD, AS YOU WOULD MAYONNAISE.

24 okra pods (about 10 ounces), stem
    ends trimmed off
1 teaspoon sea salt
1 tablespoon rice vinegar
Vegetable oil, for frying
2 ounces maifun (rice noodles) or
    Chinese saifun (bean thread noodles)
½ cup Tofu Sesame Dressing (recipe
    follows)
Shichimi (see page 14) or red pepper
    flakes (optional)

Place the okra in a bowl, add the salt and vinegar, and toss to coat. Set aside for at least 30 minutes or up to 1 hour.

Bring a medium pot of water to a boil. Add the okra, without rinsing, and cook over high heat for 1 minute, or until wilted but still bright green. Drain and set aside.

Heat ¼ inch of oil in a large heavy skillet until beginning to smoke. Add the noodles and fry until they begin to puff, about 1 minute. Using a slotted spoon plus another spoon, gather the noodles and turn them over. Continue to fry until slightly golden and puffed some more. Drain on paper towels.

To serve, transfer the okra to a bowl. Add the dressing and toss. Place the noodles on a plate, heap the dressed okra on top and serve with shichimi on the side for those who like a little extra spice.

TOFU SESAME DRESSING

3 tablespoons white sesame seeds
1 block (10 ounces) firm tofu, drained
1 tablespoon sugar
¼ teaspoon sea salt
½ tablespoon rice vinegar (optional)

Toast the sesame seeds in a dry skillet or on a microwave plate until golden and beginning to pop, about 3 to 4 minutes. Cool, then grind in a food processor, mortar with pestle, or handheld sesame seed grinder.

Place the tofu, sugar, salt, and ground sesame seeds in a food processor. Process until smooth. Stir in the vinegar, if using. Use right away. (The dressing may be refrigerated for up to 1 week.)

GREEN BEANS WITH SESAME DRESSING

SERVES 4 TO 6 AS A SIDE DISH

PUT A BEAN IN THE GROUND AND PRACTICALLY WITHOUT ATTENTION, IT RISES UP, SETS FLOWERS, AND PRODUCES SEVERAL BINS FULL OF DELICIOUS, GOOD-FOR-YOU LEGUMES. NO WONDER THE BEAN STALK IS A TOPIC OF FAIRY TALES AND ITS PRODUCE THE STUFF OF TABLES AROUND THE WORLD. THE JAPANESE LIKE THEIR GREEN BEANS AL DENTE, DEEP-FRIED AS PART OF A TEMPURA ARRAY, OR BLANCHED AND MILDLY DRESSED WITH A LIGHT SESAME DRESSING, AS HERE. THE DRESSING SUITS MANY OTHER STURDY VEGETABLES BESIDES GREEN BEANS, SUCH AS CAULIFLOWER, BROCCOLI, OR ASPARAGUS.

1 pound green beans
½ cup Sesame Dressing (recipe follows)

Bring a pot of lightly salted water to a boil. Pinch or cut the stem ends off the green beans. If the beans are small and tender, leave them whole. Cut larger beans on the diagonal into ½-inch-wide pieces. Drop the beans into the water and return to a boil. Boil the beans until barely tender and still bright green, about 1½ minutes. Drain, rinse under cool water to stop the cooking, and set aside in the drainer at room temperature for up to several hours.

When ready to serve, mound the beans in a serving dish or on individual plates and spoon the dressing over the top.

SESAME DRESSING

MAKES ½ CUP

½ cup sesame seeds
2 tablespoons sake
1 tablespoon soy sauce
1 teaspoon sugar
¼ cup Vegetable Dashi (page 37) or
  water

Toast the sesame seeds in a dry skillet or microwave plate until golden and beginning to pop, about 4 minutes. Cool, then grind in a food processor, mortar with pestle, or handheld sesame seed grinder.

Put the ground sesame seeds, sake, soy sauce, sugar, and dashi in a food processor and grind as fine as possible. Use right away or set aside at room temperature for up to several hours. (The dressing may be refrigerated for up to 3 days.)

BROCCOLI WITH SESAME AND SALTED LEMON WHEELS

❂

SERVES 4 TO 6

THE ENORMOUS WORLDWIDE CABBAGE FAMILY SHOWS UP IN JAPANESE COOKING IN THE FORM OF TURNIP, DAIKON, MUSTARD PASTE, AND CABBAGE, BUT NOT MUCH ELSE IN THE GREENS CATEGORY OTHER THAN RAPE (A MUSTARD GREEN). BROCCOLI, AN EVER AVAILABLE KIN, MIGHT AS WELL BE INCLUDED BECAUSE ITS TASTE AND TEXTURE, TO SAY NOTHING OF ITS BOTANICAL CONNECTION, FIT PERFECTLY WITH JAPANESE VEGETABLE PREPARATIONS. HERE, WILTED BROCCOLI TOPPED WITH ROUNDS OF A QUICK LEMON PICKLE AND SPRINKLED WITH SESAME SEEDS KEEPS THE SPIRIT OF THE OLD AS IT GLIMMERS WITH THE NEW.

Toast the sesame seeds in a dry skillet or microwave plate until golden and beginning to pop, about 2-3 minutes. Set aside.

Rinse the broccoli and cut off the stems, reserving the leaves. Cut the broccoli tops into florets. Peel the stems and cut them into thin rounds.

Bring a medium pot of water to boil. Add the broccoli florets, stems, and leaves and cook over high heat for 2 minutes. Drain and set aside in the drainer for 5 minutes.

While still warm, transfer the broccoli to a platter and drizzle the sesame oil over the top. Sprinkle with the sesame seeds, arrange the lemon wheels around and about, and serve.

2 teaspoons white sesame seeds

1 pound broccoli

1 teaspoon Asian sesame oil

12 Salted Lemon Wheels (recipe follows)

SALTED LEMON WHEELS

❂

MAKES 12 SLICES

Place the lemon slices on a plate. Sprinkle the salt over the slices, turn to coat both sides, and set aside for at least 20 minutes or up to several hours. Use right away. (These may be refrigerated for up to 2 days.)

1 lemon, rinsed, ends cut off, and thinly
*   sliced into 12 rounds*

1 teaspoon salt

GRILLED TOFU AND VEGETABLE SKEWERS DENGAKU

SERVES 4

ORIGINALLY GRILLED TOFU, SLATHERED ON ONE SIDE WITH DENGAKU, A SWEETENED MISO SAUCE, AND BRIEFLY REGRILLED AT THE LAST MOMENT OF COOKING, WAS A WAY TO MAKE BLAND FOOD NOT ONLY PALATABLE BUT ACTUALLY DESIRABLE. THE FORMULA WORKED SO WELL, AND THE DISH BECAME SO POPULAR THAT VENDORS POPPED UP TO OFFER THE GRILLED SNACK AND ADDED THEIR OWN INNOVATIONS WITH SKEWERS OF VEGETABLES TO ROUND OUT THE PRESENTATION. DENGAKU SKEWERS ARE NOW ORDERED IN TAKE-OUT STANDS AND VEGETARIAN RESTAURANTS FROM TOKYO TO SAN FRANCISCO BAY. WHITE MISO DENGAKU IS DECIDEDLY SWEETER THAN THE RED; THE RED IS MORE COLORFUL.

1 block (10 to 14 ounces) firm tofu

1 bell pepper, preferably red, stemmed, seeded, and cut into 1-by-2-inch pieces

2 Japanese or 1 small globe eggplant, caps cut off, Japanese eggplants halved lengthwise, regular eggplant cut into ¾-inch-thick rounds

Vegetable oil for brushing

3 small leeks, trimmed to the light green part, washed and cut crosswise into 2-inch lengths

1 cup Dengaku Sauce, white or red or a mixture (recipe follows)

Garnishes (optional)

Lightly toasted sesame seeds, black or white

Lemon zest, very finely shredded

Shredded shiso (perilla) or mint leaves

Drain the tofu block and wrap it in a kitchen towel. Set the wrapped tofu in a colander, place the colander in a bowl, and refrigerate to drain for at least 1 hour, or up to overnight.

When ready to cook, prepare a charcoal fire, allowing the coals to burn to the white stage with some red still showing through. Or preheat the broiler.

Cut the tofu into 2-inch long by ½-inch wide pieces. Insert 2 bamboo skewers, parallel to each other, in each piece. Skewer the eggplant in the same way and brush each piece lightly with oil. Skewer the bell pepper pieces, 2 pieces per skewer. Do the same with the leeks, inserting the skewer lengthwise through the pieces. (One skewer is enough to hold the pepper and leek pieces in place.)

Place the tofu and vegetable skewers on the grill and cook, turning once, until the tofu is golden on each side and the vegetables are beginning to wilt and char, about 4 minutes altogether.

Brush 1 side of each morsel with a thick coating of Dengaku Sauce, and return the skewers to the grill, sauce side up. Cook for 1 minute more, until the sauce begins to bubble.

Transfer the skewers to a serving platter. If using, sprinkle one of the garnishes over each piece, mixing and matching as you please, and serve right away.

NOTE: The timing is the same if you are broiling inside.

CHILLED TOFU WITH CONDIMENTS

SERVES 4

IN THE HEAT AND LANGUOR OF MIDSUMMER, WHEN YOUR STOMACH RUMBLES YET YOUR MUSCLES DECLINE TO MOVE AND PREPARE FOOD, CHILLED SILKEN TOFU RESOLVES THE CONFLICT IN AN ALMOST NO-EFFORT WAY. AS CENTERPIECE FOR A SIMPLE, COOLING MEAL OR STARTER FOR A MORE FORMAL OCCASION, IT SATISFIES HEARTY TO LIGHT EATERS. A BOWL OF SOY SAUCE AND SOME CONDIMENTS ARE ALL ELSE THAT'S CALLED FOR. SMALL DISHES OF GREEN ONION, GRATED GINGER, AND SLIVERED NORI ARE ESSENTIAL. AFTER THAT, YOU CAN CHOOSE TO ADD SHREDDED SHISO LEAF, JULIENNED CUCUMBER, CHIFFONADED SQUASH BLOSSOMS AS YOUR MOOD AND ENERGY DICTATE.

First, set out the condiments. Place the ginger, nori, scallions, shiso, and cucumber, if using, separately on individual serving dishes. Pour a small bowl of soy sauce for each person and set on the table.

Half fill a large serving dish with cracked ice. Cut the tofu into 1½-inch cubes and gently place the cubes on top of the ice. Garnish the tofu with the blossoms, if using, and serve right away.

4 teaspoons grated fresh ginger

½ sheet roasted nori seaweed, slivered

2 large scallions, trimmed and sliced into very thin rounds

4 shiso (perilla) leaves, finely shredded, or 2 tablespoons finely shredded celery leaves (optional)

½ Japanese cucumber, scrubbed and julienned (optional)

Soy sauce

1 pound firm tofu, preferably silken, drained and well chilled

1 large or 2 medium squash or cucumber blossoms, rinsed and finely shredded lengthwise (optional)

EGGPLANT AND SPINACH HEARTS
IN SPICY SOY AND CITRUS SAUCE

SERVES 4 TO 6

IT USED TO BE EGGPLANT CAME ONE WAY, IN LARGE, PURPLE GLOBES, MORE OR LESS ROUND, SOMETIMES A BIT ELONGATED. NOW, YOU FIND EACH SHAPE IN A MYRIAD OF COLORS AND SIZES, EACH DIFFERENTLY LABELED TO REFLECT THE CUISINE OF ITS PROMINENCE: CHINESE, THAI, GREEK, AND SO ON. THE CHOICES TESTIFY TO EGGPLANT'S UNIVERSAL APPEAL. THE JAPANESE VARIETY OF THIS NEW WORLD NIGHTSHADE VEGETABLE IS OF THE ELONGATED SORT, DARK PURPLE, ALMOST BLACK, AND NOTED FOR ITS SWEET, NOT BITTER, PULP AND TENDER SKIN, WHICH YOU DON'T HAVE TO PEEL. IT APPEARS REGULARLY AND IN MANY FORMS ON THE JAPANESE TABLE. SPINACH, TOO, HAS TAKEN ON NEW GUISES, THOUGH AN OLD-FASHIONED BUNCH OF SPINACH WITH ITS ROOTS AND TENDER BOTTOM STEMS AND HEARTS PROVIDES A TREAT THAT SHOULD NOT BE TOSSED AWAY. IN THIS RECIPE, I PAIR THE SPINACH HEARTS WITH EGGPLANT AND SPLASH THEM WITH A SPICY SOY AND CITRUS DRESSING. YOU CAN USE THE DRESSING ON ANY HEARTY VEGETABLE SALAD, FROM GRATED RED CABBAGE TO FINELY SLICED RAW FENNEL.

4 Japanese or 1 medium globe eggplant
  (about ¾ pound), trimmed and
  peeled
Sea salt
1 bunch (about ¾ pound) spinach with
  stems and roots
¼ cup vegetable oil
⅓ cup Spicy Soy and Citrus Sauce
  (recipe follows)
1 teaspoon sesame seed, toasted (optional)

Cut the eggplants into ½-inch-thick rounds. If using Japanese eggplants, leave the slices whole. If using globe eggplant, cut the slices into quarters to make smaller pieces. Place the eggplant pieces on paper towels and lightly sprinkle with salt. Turn each piece over and lightly salt the second side. Set aside to sweat and wilt for at least 45 minutes or up to 1 hour.

Cut the leaves of the spinach off the stems leaving 3 inches of stem with the roots intact. Reserve the leaves for another dish. Pull off any yellowed stems and plunge the spinach hearts in plenty of water to wash well. Lift out of the water, drain briefly, and transfer, still moist, to a medium pot. Cook over high heat for 2 minutes, turn with tongs, and continue to cook over medium-high heat for 30 seconds more, or until wilted but still bright green. Transfer to a strainer and set aside to cool.

Pour the vegetable oil into a large nonreactive frying pan and heat until smoking. Add as many eggplant pieces as will fit in 1 layer and fry, turning once, for 3 minutes, until wilted and beginning to turn golden. Transfer the cooked eggplant to paper towels and continue until all the eggplant is cooked.

Arrange the eggplant on a serving platter. Gently squeeze the spinach hearts to remove any remaining moisture and arrange them on the platter with the eggplant.

Pour the dressing over all, sprinkle with the sesame seeds, if using, and serve.

NOTE: Though not at all a Japanese cooking technique, you can bake the eggplant if you want to reduce the amount of oil required for frying. Generously oil a nonreactive baking sheet, arrange the eggplant in 1 layer on the sheet, and place in a preheated 425 degree oven. Bake for 5 minutes, turn, and bake 2 minutes more. Transfer directly to the serving platter.

SPICY SOY AND CITRUS SAUCE

MAKES ⅓ CUP

Place the oil and chili in a small pan. Heat until beginning to sizzle, then immediately lift off the burner. Stir in the lemon juice and soy sauce. Use right away or set aside for up to several hours.

1 teaspoon Asian sesame oil

½ small red chili pepper, stemmed, seeded, and finely chopped

2 tablespoons fresh lemon juice

2 tablespoons soy sauce

BRAISED GREENS AND TOFU PUFFS WITH CHRYSANTHEMUM PETALS

SERVES 4 TO 6

CHRYSANTHEMUMS ARE THE FLOWER OF AMERICAN FOOTBALL GAMES AND JAPANESE WINDOW BOXES. THEY THRIVE IN COOL AIR AND BLOOM IN THE BITE OF AUTUMN WEATHER, PROVIDING WARM COLOR AND FRAGRANCE FOR THE EYE AND PALATE ALIKE. IN FACT, THE GREENS OF A SPECIAL VARIETY ARE CULTIVATED IN JAPAN FOR TABLE USE. THE PETALS OF ANY CHRYSANTHEMUM MAY BE USED TO BRIGHTEN A DISH AND ADD THEIR OWN INDESCRIBABLE TANG. THE TOFU PUFFS ADD PROTEIN TO THE GREEENS TO COMPLETE A LIGHT FALL MEAL. SERVE WITH RICE.

2 bunches (about 1½ pounds) hardy greens, such as Chinese mustard greens, or edible chrysanthemum leaves

2 tofu puffs (aburage), sliced crosswise into ½-inch-wide pieces (see Notes)

2 cups Vegetable Dashi (page 37) or water

½ cup sake

¼ cup soy sauce

Petals from 1 yellow chrysanthemum flower, rinsed and patted dry (see Notes)

Remove the thick stems from the greens and coarsely chop the leaves. Wash the leaves, drain, and set aside without spinning dry.

Place the tofu puff slices in a bowl. Pour boiling water over, swish about, and drain. Set aside.

Combine the dashi, sake, and soy sauce in a medium saucepan. Bring to a boil, add the tofu slices, and simmer, covered, for 10 minutes, until thoroughly softened but not disintegrating. Lift out the slices with a slotted spoon and transfer them to a bowl, reserving the liquid. Set aside.

Add the greens to the pot and stir over medium-high heat until thoroughly wilted and softened but still bright green, 3 to 4 minutes. Transfer the greens and remaining liquid to a serving bowl. Add the tofu puff slices and sprinkle the flower petals over the top. Serve right away.

NOTES: You can substitute sliced shiitake mushrooms for the tofu puffs. Substitute nasturtium petals or lemon zest for the chrysanthemum petals.

CHAPTER SIX

SWEETS

DULCET TASTES TO END THE MEAL

THE DAILY JAPANESE MEAL ENDS WITH A BOWL OF STEAMING RICE, TINY SIDE DISHES OF PICKLED VEGETABLES, AND A CUP OF HOT GREEN TEA. For special occasions and banquets, sweets are offered: cakes, dumplings, and buns of rice flour; sweetened beans as porridge or paste; some fruit, either fresh or canned; and, most recently, green tea—not hot in a cup, but cold in an ice cream. While sugared beans and not very sweet cakes may seem odd ways to finish the meal, the tastes, textures, and combinations work in a satisfying and most interesting way. Following is an eclectic set of desserts based on traditional Japanese elements, but put together in a modern, Western cook's style. Dessert, after all, is just for fun.

AZUKI BEANS, SAVORY AND SWEET

❀

MAKES 2 CUPS COOKED BEANS

RECIPE BASICS FOR BEANS ARE NOT NORMALLY FOUND IN THE DESSERT SECTION OF A COOKERY BOOK, BUT THE PLACEMENT HERE SUITS JAPANESE CUISINE. THAT'S BECAUSE THE SMALL, RED AZUKI BEANS, AN OLD WORLD VARIETY NOT AT ALL THE SAME AS THE NEW WORLD KIDNEY BEANS OF TEXAS CHILI AND LOUISIANA RED BEANS AND RICE, ARE CUSTOMARILY SWEETENED AND ONLY SECONDARILY EMPLOYED IN SAVORY DISHES. THE TRADITIONAL WAY TO COOK RED BEANS IS TO PUT THEM IN THE POT WITHOUT SOAKING. MORE WATER IS ADDED ALONG THE WAY AS THE BEANS SOAK UP THE LIQUID. I PREFER A QUICK PRESOAK, WITH ALL THE WATER ADDED AT THE OUTSET. IT'S LESS FUSS FOR THE COOK, AND I FIND THE BEANS TURN OUT MORE TENDER WHEN COOKED THIS WAY. USE THE SAVORY VERSION IN SMALL AMOUNTS, A DISCREET BEAN OR TWO OR THREE HERE AND THERE FOR APPETIZER OR DINNER DISHES. USE THE SWEET VERSION — WITH ITS DAUNTING AMOUNT OF SUGAR — FOR THE CLASSIC *ZENZAI* (PAGE 121), PUREE THEM FOR FILLING OTHER KINDS OF SWEET CONCOCTIONS, OR SIMPLY TOP VANILLA ICE CREAM WITH A SPOONFUL.

Put the beans and 3 cups of water in a medium pot. Bring to a boil, remove from the heat, and set aside to soak for 1 hour.

Drain the beans and put them in a clean pot with 5 cups of water. Bring to a boil and simmer briskly, uncovered, for 45 minutes, or until soft all the way through but not disintegrating.

For savory beans, stir in the salt and remove from the heat. Use right away or cool and refrigerate in the cooking liquid. (Savory beans may be refrigerated for up to several weeks.)

For sweet bean porridge, add the salt and the sugar and continue to simmer briskly for 10 minutes more. Remove from the heat and use right away, or cool and refrigerate in the cooking liquid. (Sweet bean porridge may be refrigerated for up to several weeks.)

¾ cup (6 ounces) azuki beans

¼ teaspoon sea salt

1½ cups sugar, if making sweet porridge

RED BEAN PORRIDGE WITH SWEET
RICE DUMPLINGS AND BLOOD ORANGES

SERVES 4

So fascinating the name *ZENZAI,* so basic the ingredients, and so classic in Japanese cuisine is the combination of sweet beans and rice for dessert, that it must be included in this volume. Usually, a small bowlful serves as a lovely way to end a light meal, but it could almost be a meal in itself for those with a sweet tooth. For pizzazz this rendition has decorative slices of blood orange in the tradition of *MUKIMONO,* the Japanese art of cutting vegetables and fruit into decorative shapes.

Rinse the orange. Cut off the skin and membrane and slice the orange into 8 rounds and set aside.

Place about ¼ cup of the porridge plus some of the porridge juices in 4 individual bowls. Place 2 rice dumplings in each bowl and arrange the orange rounds around the beans and dumplings. Garnish with the orange loops and serve.

1 blood orange

1 cup red bean porridge (see page 119)

8 Sweet Rice Dumplings (page 124)

*8 Decorative Orange Loops, preferably
from a blood orange (recipe follows)*

DECORATIVE ORANGE LOOPS

MAKES 8 TO 10 LOOPS

Rinse the orange and cut off the ends. Without peeling, cut the orange in half lengthwise. Cut each half crosswise into ⅜-inch thick half slices.

With a paring knife, cut the skin and white membrane of each slice from the pulp, leaving ½-inch still attached. Curl the free end of the skin under to make a loop at the top of each slice.

If the orange rind is too thick to tuck under without popping back up, pare away some of the white part so it easily folds into a curl. Use to decorate as desired.

1 orange

TOASTED AND SUGARED MOCHI CAKES WITH CHESTNUTS IN SYRUP

✿

SERVES 4 TO 6

MOCHI CAKES, ROUNDS OR SQUARES OF STEAMED AND POUNDED GLUTINOUS RICE THAT LOOK A BIT LIKE SMALL HOCKEY PUCKS OR TILES OF EXOTIC SOAP, ALWAYS APPEAR AS A SWEET OR SAVORY TREAT AT NEW YEAR'S CELEBRATIONS. DENSE AND SEEMINGLY HEAVY, THE CAKES ARE TRANSFORMED INTO LIGHT AND AIRY PUFFS WHEN BROILED OR TOASTED. FOR A SWEET TREATMENT, THE PUFFS GET A DULCET FILLING, LIKE CHESTNUTS IN SYRUP, ANOTHER TRADITIONAL OFFERING FOR NEW YEAR'S. ONE EACH OF THESE CONFECTIONS IS AMPLE. FOR TEA, PERHAPS TWO EACH. YOU CAN FIND MOCHI CAKES IN JAPANESE MARKETS, FRESH AROUND NEW YEAR'S OR FROZEN AT OTHER TIMES OF THE YEAR. • BESIDES TOPPING AND MOISTENING MOCHI CAKES, HOMEMADE CHESTNUTS IN SYRUP ARE SPECIAL ENOUGH TO SERVE ALONE WITHOUT FURTHER ADO. PLACE THREE PER PERSON IN INDIVIDUAL BOWLS, SPOON OVER SOME OF THE SYRUP, AND ENJOY THE NEW YEAR.

---

8 mochi cakes; rounds or 2-inch squares

2 tablespoons powdered sugar

12 Chestnuts in Syrup (recipe follows; see Note)

Place the cakes in a hot oven or under the broiler. Toast them until they begin to puff up, 1-4 minutes, depending on the freshness. Turn them and continue toasting until they are golden and beginning to split apart, 1 or 2 minutes more.

Make a lengthwise slit in the top of each cake and sift powdered sugar over them. Place the cakes on individual serving plates, one or two for each plate. Insert 1 or 2 chestnuts in the center of each cake and spoon some of the chestnut syrup over the top. Serve right away once toasted; the cakes do not keep.

NOTE: Red bean porridge (see page 119) can be used to fill the mochi cakes in place of the chestnuts.

CHESTNUTS IN SYRUP

✿

MAKES 2 CUPS

½ pound (18 to 20) fresh chestnuts (see page 63)

¾ cup sugar

¼ cup sake

Combine the sugar, sake, and 1 cup of water in a small pot. Bring to a boil and simmer for 10 minutes, or until thickened.

Drop in the chestnuts, bring back to a boil, and simmer briskly for 15 minutes, or until the liquid is thick enough to coat a spoon and the chestnuts are cooked but still whole. Remove from the heat and use right away. (The chestnuts may be refrigerated in the syrup almost indefinitely.)

SWEET RICE DUMPLINGS

FROM EVERY BOOK I WRITE COME TWO OR THREE DISCOVERIES I CARRY FORWARD IN MY DAILY COOKING. ONE SUCH IS THIS SWEET RICE DUMPLING. IT'S LIGHT AND AIRY AND QUICK AS A WINK TO MAKE AT HOME. THE "SWEET" PART OF ITS NAME REFERS TO THE GLUTINOUS RICE FLOUR IT'S MADE FROM. YOU CAN MAKE THE DUMPLINGS SWEETER STILL AND SITUATE THEM IN A BOWL OF FRUIT OR INCLUDE THEM WITH RED BEAN PORRIDGE FOR THE CLASSIC *ZENZAI* (SEE PAGE 121). OR, YOU CAN TURN THE DUMPLINGS SAVORY BY REPLACING THE SUGAR WITH A QUARTER TEASPOON SALT AND MIXING IN TWO TEASPOONS MINCED SCALLION, THEN SERVE THE SAVORY ONES IN A MORE WESTERN STYLE, LIKE GNOCCHI, OR FLOAT THEM IN SOUP.

⅓ cup sweet rice flour (mochiko; see page 11)

1 teaspoon sugar (see Notes)

Place the flour and sugar in a small bowl. Stir in 2 tablespoons water and knead the mixture with your hands a few seconds to make a soft, smooth dough. Divide the dough into 8 portions. Roll each portion between the palms of your hands to make a cherry-sized ball. Slightly flatten each ball between your thumb and forefinger, making a small indentation at the top and bottom of the ball. Set the dumplings aside on a plate as you go.

Bring a medium pot of water to a boil. Drop in the dumplings and boil briskly until they rise to the top, 1½ to 2 minutes, depending on the size of the pot and amount of water. With a slotted spoon, transfer the dumplings to a damp towel. Use right away or set aside for up to 30 minutes, but no longer. After that the dumplings harden and become gluey.

NOTES: Japanese cooks do not further sweeten the already sweet glutinous rice dough, but I find a touch of sugar in the mix makes them even tastier.

The recipe can be doubled. Don't be tempted, though, to roll the dumplings larger, or the centers will remain uncooked while the outside disintegrates.

HACHIYA PERSIMMON JELLY WITH
FUYU PERSIMMON SLICES

SERVES 8 TO 12

THE DENSE, CANDY-LIKE GELATIN DESSERT CALLED *YOKAN* TYPIFIES THE "LITTLE SWEET TASTE" THAT MIGHT END A JAPANESE MEAL. IT'S A PUREE OF SWEETENED RED BEANS OR SOFT FRUIT THICKENED WITH AGAR-AGAR. THE RESULTING CONFECTION HAS A TEXTURE SOMEWHERE BETWEEN AN AMERICAN JELL-O AND A MEXICAN FRUIT PASTE. HACHIYA PERSIMMON, READY TO SAVOR ONLY WHEN ITS PULP HAS RIPENED INTO A JAMLIKE VISCOSITY SOFT ENOUGH TO SPOON, MAKES A NATURAL BASE FOR YOKAN. FUYU PERSIMMON, A DIFFERENT VARIETY OF THE SAME FRUIT THAT'S READY TO EAT WHILE STILL FIRM — LIKE AN APPLE OR A PEAR — SLICES INTO A PERFECT GARNISH FOR THE PERSIMMON YOKAN. THE TWO REDOUBLE THE FLAVOR OF THIS UNIQUE WINTER FRUIT. AGAR-AGAR IS AVAILABLE IN JAPANESE AND CHINESE MARKETS IN PACKAGES CONTAINING WHAT LOOK LIKE RECTANGULAR COLUMNS OF MATERIALS PERHAPS SUITABLE FOR PACKING DELICATE OBJECTS FOR SHIPPING. AGAR-AGAR IS OF SPECIAL INTEREST TO THE VEGETARIAN COOK: IT'S A VEGETABLE PRODUCT THAT REPLACES THE STANDARD GELATIN (AN ANIMAL PRODUCT) OR OLD-FASHIONED ISINGLASS (A FISH PRODUCT) FOR ANY JELLYING NEEDS YOU MAY HAVE.

Peel the Hachiya persimmons, remove any seeds, and puree the pulp. Transfer the pureed pulp to a medium bowl and stir in the lemon juice. Set aside.

Break the agar-agar into pieces and place them in a bowl. Cover with enough water to float the pieces, place a plate on top to keep them submerged, and set aside to soak and soften for 20 minutes.

Lift out the agar-agar pieces and squeeze out the excess water. Place the agar-agar, the sugar, and 2½ cups of water in a small pot. Bring to a boil over medium-high heat and simmer for 3 minutes, stirring from time to time to help break up the pieces. Strain the agar-agar into the bowl with the persimmon puree. Set the bowl into a larger bowl partially filled with ice water and stir until the mixture cools to room temperature.

Strain the persimmon mixture into a rectangular or square baking pan. Cover and refrigerate until set into a jelly, about 1½ hours.

When ready to serve, loosen the jelly by inserting a knife between it and the container. Invert the entire mold onto a plate and cut into 12 squares. Place 1 or 2 squares on individual plates and garnish each plate with Fuyu persimmon rounds. Serve.

3 large (1½ lbs) very ripe Hachiya persimmons
1 tablespoon fresh lemon juice
1 stick agar-agar
⅓ cup sugar
2 medium Fuyu persimmons, peeled and cut into ⅛-inch-thick rounds

GREEN TEA AND SHISO GRANITA
WITH FRESH CHERRIES

❦

SERVES 4 TO 6

I F ANYTHING COULD REPLACE THE NEW DESSERT STAPLE OF JAPANESE RESTAURANT FARE, GREEN TEA ICE CREAM, IT WOULD BE GREEN TEA GRANITA. THE DRAWBACK IS THAT AN ICE CREAM MAKER IS NO HELP HERE. GRANITA MAKING REQUIRES PATIENCE AS YOU ATTEND THE PROCESS, STIRRING FROM TIME TO TIME TO BREAK UP THE CHILLING CRYSTALS AS THE ICE FREEZES. IT IS VERY MUCH A ZEN EXERCISE. THE CHERRIES ARE SPECIAL, TOO. CHERRIES ARE ACCLAIMED AND PRAISED IN JAPANESE LIFE, AND EACH SPRING THEY APPEAR IN CHERRY BLOSSOM RICE, CHERRY BLOSSOM MOCHI, AND CHERRY BLOSSOM FESTIVALS APLENTY. BUT WHERE IS THE BOWL OF CHERRIES? IF THEY'RE SERVED ON THEIR OWN AT ALL IN JAPAN, THEY COME FROM A CAN OR JAR OF PRESERVED ONES, PERHAPS BECAUSE THE CHERRY SEASON IS SO SHORT-LIVED AND THE CROP SO LIMITED. IN AMERICAN MARKETS, THOUGH, FRESH CHERRIES ARE AVAILABLE FROM LATE SPRING THROUGH EARLY SUMMER. A MOUND OF THEM IN A BOWL WITH GREEN TEA GRANITA IS NOTHING LESS THAN OPULENT. IT SEEMS A FITTING WAY TO END THIS VOLUME.

2 tablespoons Japanese green tea

6 green shiso (perilla) leaves (see Note)

¾ cup sugar

3 cups boiling water

1 pound fresh cherries, rinsed

Place the tea, shiso leaves, and sugar in a medium bowl. Add the water, stir to dissolve the sugar, and set aside to steep for 5 minutes. Strain into a clean bowl and set aside to cool to room temperature.

Stir again and place the bowl in the freezer until the mixture begins to chill around the edges and across the top, about 1 hour. Whisk to break up and mix in the ice crystals. Return the bowl to the freezer and chill for 2 hours more.

Whisk again, breaking up the crystals and stirring to make an evenly granulated mixture. Return to the freezer until frozen again, but not hard as a rock. Use right away or cover and keep in the freezer. (The granita may be frozen for up to several days.)

When ready to serve, remove the bowl from the freezer and set aside at room temperature until the granita softens enough to spoon out, about 45 minutes.

Place 3 scoops of the granita in individual serving bowls. Divide the cherries, among the bowls.

NOTE: To maintain the fresh herb flavor and aroma of the granita if you don't have shiso, you can substitute 6 large mint leaves.

INDEX

TABLE OF EQUIVALENTS

THE EXACT EQUIVALENTS IN THE FOLLOWING TABLES HAVE

BEEN ROUNDED FOR CONVENIENCE.

LIQUID AND DRY MEASURES
U.S. METRIC

¼ teaspoon	1.25 milliliters
½ teaspoon	2.5 milliliters
1 teaspoon	5 milliliters
1 tablespoon (3 tsp)	15 milliliters
1 fluid ounce (2 tbsp)	30 milliliters
¼ cup	60 milliliters
⅓ cup	80 milliliters
1 cup	240 milliliters
1 pint (2 cups)	480 milliliters
1 quart (4 cups, 32 oz)	960 milliliters
1 gallon (4 quarts)	3.84 liters
1 ounce (by weight)	28 grams
1 pound	454 grams
2.2 pounds	1 kilogram

LENGTH MEASURES
U.S. METRIC

⅛ inch	3 millimeters
¼ inch	6 millimeters
½ inch	12 millimeters
1 inch	2.5 centimeters

OVEN TEMPERATURES

Fahrenheit	Celsius	Gas
250	120	½
275	140	1
300	150	2
325	160	3
350	180	4
375	190	5
400	200	6
425	220	7
450	230	8
475	240	9
500	260	10